EMPOWERING HABITS FOR WORKPLACE SUCCESS

THE ESSENTIAL GUIDE TO BUILDING FULFILLING CAREER

SCOTT E SALSBURY

Copyright © [2024] by Scott e Salsbury

All rights reserved. No part of this book may be reproduced, stored in a retrieval system, or transmitted in any form or by any means, electronic, mechanical, photocopying, recording, or otherwise, without the prior written permission of the publisher, except for brief quotations used in reviews or scholarly works.

Disclaimer: The information provided in this book is intended for educational and informational purposes only. The author and publisher are not engaged in rendering professional services. Readers are advised to seek professional guidance specific to their circumstances. Feel free to modify the details to fit the specific needs of your book.

TABLE OF CONTENTS

INTRODUCTION   6
   UNDERSTANDING THE ROLE OF HABITS IN SUCCESS   10
   HOW POSITIVE HABITS SHAPE CAREERS   16

CHAPTER 1   24

SETTING CLEAR GOALS AND INTENTIONS   24
   THE RESEARCH BEHIND REACHING YOUR OBJECTIVES   31
   MATCHING PERSONAL VALUES WITH CAREER CHOICES   40
   SIMPLIFYING COMPLEX GOALS INTO MANAGEABLE CHUNKS   47

CHAPTER 2   53

MASTERING TIME MANAGEMENT   53
   PRIORITIZATION TECHNIQUES FOR PEAK PRODUCTIVITY   59
   MANAGING DISTRACTIONS AND STAYING Focused   66
   BUILDING CONSISTENT DAILY ROUTINES   72

CHAPTER 3   80

BUILDING EFFECTIVE COMMUNICATION SKILLS   80
   ACTIVE LISTENING FOR BETTER UNDERSTANDING   88
   SPEAKING WITH CLARITY AND CONFIDENCE

94		
	NAVIGATING CHALLENGING CONVERSATIONS	100
CHAPTER		**104**
4		**104**
DEVELOPING A GROWTH MINDSET		**105**
	EMBRACING CHALLENGES AS OPPORTUNITIES	111
	LEARNING FROM FEEDBACK AND MISTAKES	117
	CULTIVATING RESILIENCE IN THE WORKPLACE	123
CHAPTER		**128**
5		**128**
FOSTERING COLLABORATION AND TEAMWORK		**129**
	BUILDING TRUST WITHIN TEAMS	137
	EFFECTIVE DELEGATION AND FEEDBACK	145
	COMPASSIONATE CONFLICT MANAGEMENT	154
CHAPTER		**162**
6		**162**
DEVELOPING SELF AWARENESS AND SOCIAL SKILLS FOR PERSONAL GROWTH		**163**
	RECOGNIZING AND MANAGING EMOTIONAL RESPONSES	171
	USING EMPATHY TO STRENGTHEN CONNECTIONS	178
	MANAGING STRESS IN HIGH-PRESSURE SITUATIONS	184
CHAPTER		**189**

7

MANAGING STRESS AND AVOIDING BURNOUT — 189

   RECOGNIZING SIGNS OF STRESS EARLY — 197
   PRACTICING MINDFULNESS AND RELAXATION — 203
   ACHIEVING WORK-LIFE BALANCE — 210

CHAPTER 8

HARNESSING CREATIVITY AND INNOVATION — 218

   THINKING OUTSIDE THE BOX IN PROBLEM-SOLVING — 226
   EMBRACING CHANGE AND STAYING AGILE — 235
   LEVERAGING INNOVATION TO STAND OUT — 244

CHAPTER 9

BUILDING A PROFESSIONAL IMAGE AND REPUTATION — 253

   DEVELOPING TRUST AND CREDIBILITY — 262
   NETWORKING WITH PURPOSE — 269
   USING SOCIAL MEDIA FOR CAREER ADVANCEMENT — 278

CHAPTER 10

BECOMING A LIFELONG LEARNER — 286

   THE IMPORTANCE OF CONTINUOUS EDUCATION — 296

- SEEKING MENTORSHIP AND LEARNING OPPORTUNITIES ... 304
- STAYING RELEVANT IN A COMPETITIVE INDUSTRY ... 313

CHAPTER 11 ... 322

THE ROLE OF SELF-CARE IN SUSTAINING SUCCESS ... 322

- THE IMPACT OF PHYSICAL HEALTH ON PERFORMANCE ... 332
- SUPPORTING MENTAL WELLNESS ... 337
- BALANCING WORK AND PERSONAL GROWTH ... 346

CHAPTER 12 ... 353

BUILDING HABITS THAT LAST ... 355

- STRATEGIES FOR MAINTAINING POSITIVE CHANGES ... 362
- OVERCOMING CHALLENGES IN HABIT FORMATION ... 371
- CELEBRATING WINS TO STAY MOTIVATED ... 379

CONCLUSION ... 387

- THE POWER OF CONSISTENCY AND COMMITMENT ... 391
- EMBRACING THE JOURNEY OF GROWTH ... 395
- ACKNOWLEDGMENTS ... 399

INTRODUCTION

UNLOCKING THE POWER OF WORKPLACE HABITS

In the early 20th century, a pioneering industrialist and founder of a renowned automotive company revolutionized the manufacturing process by introducing the assembly line.

What made this innovation transformative wasn't just the machinery—it was the disciplined habits ingrained in workers that ensured consistency, efficiency, and progress.

This simple yet powerful concept—habitual excellence—has driven remarkable achievements across centuries.

The success of individuals and organizations has often hinged on one common thread: empowering habits that foster productivity, resilience, and adaptability.

Imagine walking into an office where chaos reigns. Papers are scattered, meetings run late, and tasks pile up. Now picture another office—calm, organized, and productive.

Employees here know their priorities, meet deadlines effortlessly, and seem genuinely satisfied. The difference? It's not intelligence, talent, or luck—it's the empowering habits they've built.

Habits are like the invisible gears of a machine; if they're well-oiled, the entire system runs smoothly. If not, even the most skilled workers face setbacks. Now, Which type of office setting do you think you'd thrive in?

What separates workplace success from mediocrity? Is it just about working harder or having a higher level of mental ability? The solution can be found in developing positive and uplifting habits that promote growth and improvement.

Habits are the hidden foundation of success, transforming ordinary actions into extraordinary outcomes.

Whether you're aiming for leadership, collaboration, or personal growth, mastering the right habits unlocks unparalleled opportunities.

The best part? Anyone can build these habits with intention and consistency. What could change in your career if you mastered habits that lead to peak performance?

Do you want to break free from workplace stress and inefficiency? Are you prepared to tap into your inner strength and accomplish the goals you've always dreamed of?

Empowering Habits for Workplace Success is your guide to mastering the habits that transform ordinary careers into exceptional journeys.

Filled with valuable advice, tested techniques, and useful guidance, this book provides you with the essential resources to succeed and flourish.

Whether you're an aspiring leader, a team player, or a seasoned professional, this book will reshape the way you approach work.

Don't just dream of success—build it, one empowering habit at a time. Let's embark on this journey together!

UNDERSTANDING THE ROLE OF HABITS IN SUCCESS

Cassandra Peter was a young professional, fresh out of college, and brimming with potential. However, her days were a whirlwind of missed deadlines, forgotten commitments, and overwhelming stress.

Her career appeared to be stagnant, trapped in a cycle of average performance.

One day, a mentor pulled her aside and asked, "What does your morning look like?" Cassandra Peter's brow furrowed in bewilderment as she attempted to find a connection between the question and her assessment.

Her mentor smiled knowingly and replied, "Habits define success, Cassandra Peter. Master your day by mastering the little things."

Intrigued, Cassandra Peter began by making small changes—waking up at the same time each day, planning her priorities, and sticking to a set routine. Slowly, she noticed a shift.

Deadlines were met with ease, her creativity flourished, and colleagues began to seek her advice. The change wasn't drastic—it was gradual but profound.

Cassandra Peter realized that by cultivating empowering habits, she had unlocked the door to workplace success.

"Habits are the architects of our destiny. What we repeatedly do shapes not only our achievements but the very essence of who we are.

To succeed in the workplace, empower yourself with intentional actions, for success is not an event—it is a series of deliberate, consistent choices."

Habits are the unseen forces that guide our daily thoughts and actions. They are the automatic behaviors we perform without conscious thought, yet they hold immense power in shaping our personal and professional success.

In the workplace, habits can either propel you forward or hold you back. Understanding their role is key to thriving in your career.

1. Consistency Builds Trust and Reliability

Consistent habits, such as punctuality, meeting deadlines, and delivering quality work, establish you as a reliable team member.

Colleagues and leaders value individuals who can be counted on to perform consistently, making habits the foundation of trust in professional relationships.

2. Efficiency Through Routine

Establishing predictable routines streamlines your decision-making process, freeing up cognitive energy for imaginative and tactical thinking.

Simple habits like organizing your workspace, planning tasks ahead, and adhering to a schedule can dramatically improve productivity and focus.

3. Skill Development Through Repetition

Success often hinges on mastering key skills. Habits like dedicating 20 minutes daily to learning a new tool or refining a specific skill compound over time.

This consistent effort builds expertise and positions you as a valuable asset in your workplace.

4. Cultivating a Growth Mindset

Empowering habits extend beyond actions to how we think. Practices like daily reflection, seeking feedback, and setting incremental goals foster a growth mindset.

This perspective encourages you to view challenges as opportunities, which is critical for long-term success.

5. Breaking Limiting Patterns

Identifying and substituting counterproductive behaviors is equally vital. Procrastination, negative self-talk, or lack of organization can hinder progress. Replacing these with proactive and positive habits sets the stage for success.

HOW POSITIVE HABITS SHAPE CAREERS

Picture your career as a vibrant garden. Every day, you have the opportunity to plant seeds—small actions and habits that, over time, bloom into a lush landscape of success.

Now, think of positive habits as the water and sunlight your garden craves. Without them, your potential withers.

Perhaps your "watering can" is prioritizing tasks each morning, ensuring every plant (or project) gets the attention it needs.

Maybe your "sunlight" is the glow of gratitude you show to coworkers, encouraging your career to grow in unexpected ways.

But beware! Neglecting habits like effective communication or learning new skills is like letting weeds take over.

One day you're ignoring an email; the next, your reputation is overrun with missed opportunities.

When stress storms roll in, the roots of strong habits keep your garden grounded. A mindful pause—a few moments to breathe and refocus—is like a gardener pruning overgrowth after the rain.

The best part? Your thriving garden inspires others. When teammates see your diligence, positivity, and commitment, they start planting their own seeds, and soon the entire workplace blossoms with productivity and harmony.

So, are you ready to grab your tools and cultivate a flourishing career garden? Start small, nurture daily, and watch your career transform into something truly extraordinary.

In the fast-paced modern workplace, habits play a pivotal role in shaping career trajectories. The habits we cultivate not only define how we manage our tasks but also influence how others perceive us.

Building empowering habits can lead to workplace success by fostering productivity, enhancing relationships, and aligning actions with long-term goals.

- **The Power of Routine in Professional Growth**

Consistency is a cornerstone of success, and positive habits create a foundation for consistent performance.

Establishing routines such as starting the day with a clear plan or practicing effective time management allows professionals to tackle challenges methodically.

These habits reduce decision fatigue, freeing mental energy for high-value tasks and strategic thinking.

For instance, dedicating the first 30 minutes of your workday to prioritizing tasks ensures that essential responsibilities receive attention before distractions arise.

This habit, when practiced consistently, builds a reputation for reliability and efficiency.

- **Communication Habits That Build Trust**

Positive communication habits can significantly impact workplace relationships.

Responding to emails promptly, listening actively during meetings, and showing appreciation for colleagues' contributions foster an environment of mutual respect.

These habits not only enhance collaboration but also position you as a team player and leader.

For example, instead of multitasking during conversations, focusing entirely on the speaker signals respect and engagement.

Over time, this habit strengthens professional bonds and opens doors for career advancement.

- **Lifelong Learning as a Habit**

In a constantly evolving job market, the habit of lifelong learning is crucial. Committing to ongoing personal and professional development keeps skills sharp and relevant.

Whether through online courses, reading industry-related materials, or seeking mentorship, learning ensures adaptability to changes and innovations.

Setting aside even 20 minutes a day to acquire new knowledge compounds over time, positioning you as an expert in your field.

This habit also demonstrates to employers and peers that you are invested in growth and willing to evolve with industry trends.

- **Managing Stress with Positive Habits**

Workplace challenges often come with stress, but positive habits can help mitigate its impact.

Practicing mindfulness, maintaining a healthy work-life balance, and setting realistic boundaries ensure mental clarity and resilience.

For example, a habit as simple as taking short, mindful breaks throughout the day can improve focus and prevent burnout.

- **Leading by Example**

In leadership roles, habits have a cascading effect on team culture. When leaders exhibit discipline, empathy, and a commitment to excellence, their teams often mirror these behaviors.

Positive habits like acknowledging team efforts, maintaining transparency, and embracing feedback build trust and loyalty, essential for collective success.

CHAPTER

1

SETTING CLEAR GOALS AND INTENTIONS

Clarity of purpose is the cornerstone of success—when you set clear goals, you define your destination, and with focused intentions, you chart the path.

In the workplace, this alignment transforms effort into impact, challenges into opportunities, and aspirations into achievements.

Success isn't just reaching the goal; it's the journey of purpose-driven actions that create lasting growth and fulfillment.

In the journey toward workplace success, one of the most empowering habits is setting clear goals and intentions.

These act as the compass that directs your actions, ensuring you stay focused on what truly matters.

Without clear goals, efforts can become scattered, leading to wasted energy and diminished outcomes.

- **Why Goals and Intentions Matter**

Goals serve as a guiding target, while intentions instill your actions with direction, significance, and drive.

Together, they create a framework that boosts productivity, fosters accountability, and enhances overall satisfaction in your work.

When aligned with personal and organizational values, goals and intentions help ensure every step you take contributes to meaningful progress.

- **Defining Your Goals**

1. Be Specific: Avoid vague statements like "I want to be better at my job." Instead, specify what "better" means—for instance, "I will improve my client communication skills to increase satisfaction ratings by 15% this quarter."

2. Make Goals Measurable: Quantify your objectives so you can track progress. This could include timelines, numerical targets, or milestones.

3. Stay Realistic: While it's great to aim high, goals should be achievable within the context of your resources and time.

4. Ensure Relevance: Align your goals with your role, team objectives, and long-term career aspirations.

5. Create a Schedule with Specific Due Dates: Deadlines attached to goals create a motivating sense of urgency, prompting timely progress.

- **Crafting Strong Intentions**

Unlike goals, which focus on results, intentions are rooted in how you approach your work. Setting intentions establishes a mindset that shapes your day-to-day actions.

- **Example of a Goal:** "Complete the quarterly report by the 15th to meet the scheduled deadline."

- **Example of an Intention:** "Compile a detailed analytical report that applies data-driven knowledge to strategic planning, optimizes decision-making processes, and facilitates seamless implementation."

Intentions provide the emotional and mental energy behind achieving your goals.

They help you remain positive, adaptable, and motivated, even when challenges arise.

- **Steps to Implement Goals and Intentions in the Workplace**

1. Write Them Down: Documenting your goals and intentions solidifies your commitment and provides a reference point for progress.

2. Dissect Goals into Achievable Milestones: Achieve big goals by dividing them into smaller, manageable chunks, and maintain momentum.

3. Communicate Goals with Stakeholders: Sharing your goals with colleagues or supervisors fosters collaboration and accountability.

4. Review and Adjust Regularly: Workplace dynamics often shift. Periodically assess your goals and intentions to ensure they remain relevant.

5. Celebrate Milestones: Acknowledge your achievements along the way to sustain motivation.

- **Overcoming Obstacles**

It's common to encounter setbacks while pursuing goals. To stay on track:

- Reassess and redefine your goals if necessary.

- Use failures as learning opportunities.

- Stay rooted in your intentions to maintain focus and resilience.

THE RESEARCH BEHIND REACHING YOUR OBJECTIVES

Have you noticed how some individuals easily attain their objectives, while others face difficulties in moving forward? The truth is discovered not in luck, but in science-backed habits and strategies that anyone can adopt.

What if you could transform your daily routine to not only meet your objectives but exceed them with confidence and clarity?

This isn't just another list of workplace tips—it's a deep dive into the proven research that makes goal-setting, habit formation, and productivity attainable for everyone.

Imagine being equipped with tools that help you unlock hidden potential, improve focus, and conquer challenges, all while feeling more fulfilled in your career.

If you're ready to discover how small changes can lead to massive success, how mindfulness can reshape your approach to stress, and why celebrating even the smallest wins can build unstoppable momentum, then this is your guide.

You'll learn about the science of habits, the power of a growth mindset, and actionable strategies tailored for real workplace challenges.

Keep reading to turn knowledge into empowerment and move one step closer to mastering the art of workplace success. Your goals are attainable – let's begin the journey to make them happen.

Reaching your workplace objectives is a science as much as an art. Groundbreaking studies in psychology, productivity, and behavioral science provide valuable insights into how habits shape professional success.

Here, we dive into the research-backed principles that empower individuals to achieve their goals effectively in the workplace.

1. The Habit Loop: Cue, Routine, Reward

Behavioral scientists have identified a pattern known as the "habit loop" that governs how habits form and influence outcomes. This loop consists of three elements:

- **Cue:** A trigger that initiates a behavior.

- **Routine:** The action you take.

- **Reward:** The positive reinforcement that encourages repetition.

For workplace success, understanding and optimizing this loop can lead to creating habits like punctuality, proactive communication, and focused work sessions.

For example, setting a morning alarm (cue), engaging in a brief planning session (routine), and experiencing clarity for the day (reward) strengthens productivity.

2. Goal Setting: SMART Framework

Achieving objectives begins with clear, actionable goals. Research suggests that the SMART framework—Specific, Measurable, Achievable, Relevant, and Time-bound—enhances the likelihood of success.

By breaking down broader objectives into manageable milestones, individuals can maintain motivation and track progress effectively.

For instance, Replace ambiguous goals, such as 'improve time management,' with specific objectives, like 'decrease non-essential activities by 20% within the next month."

3. The Role of Keystone Habits

Certain habits, known as keystone habits, have a cascading effect, transforming other aspects of life and work.

A study by Charles Duhigg highlights how habits like regular exercise or consistent scheduling can lead to improved discipline, enhanced focus, and better emotional regulation in the workplace.

By identifying and cultivating keystone habits, professionals can unlock higher levels of efficiency and adaptability.

4. Mindfulness and Its Impact on Performance

Mindfulness—a state of focused awareness of the present—has been linked to improved concentration, reduced stress, and enhanced problem-solving skills.

Workplace studies show that mindfulness practices, such as meditation or journaling, can increase productivity by helping individuals navigate challenges with a calm, clear mind.

Integrating short mindfulness breaks into your day can act as a mental reset, boosting creativity and resilience.

5. The Science of Small Wins

Teresa Amabile's research on motivation reveals the power of small wins.

Incremental progress toward a goal creates a sense of accomplishment that fuels further efforts.

Acknowledging these achievements, even if minor, builds momentum and reinforces positive behaviors.

For example, celebrating the completion of daily tasks or weekly targets fosters a culture of success and confidence.

6. Social Accountability and Collaboration

Studies emphasize the importance of social connections and accountability in reaching objectives.

Sharing goals with colleagues or mentors and collaborating on team projects increases commitment and fosters mutual support.

Additionally, environments that encourage open communication and feedback tend to cultivate more engaged and productive professionals.

7. The Power of Positive Reinforcement

Positive reinforcement, as highlighted by B.F. Skinner's behavioral studies are a powerful motivator.

Recognizing and rewarding desirable actions—whether through verbal praise, performance bonuses, or personal treats—encourages repeated success-oriented behaviors.

8. Neuroplasticity and the Growth Mindset

The concept of neuroplasticity—the brain's ability to rewire itself based on experiences—shows that habits and behaviors can change over time.

Carol Dweck's research on the growth mindset further supports this, emphasizing that individuals who view challenges as opportunities for growth are more likely to achieve their goals.

Adopting this mindset can transform setbacks into learning opportunities, fostering resilience and continuous improvement.

- **Implementing Research-Driven Strategies for Success**

Understanding the science behind habits and workplace success empowers individuals to create systems tailored to their unique goals and environments.

MATCHING PERSONAL VALUES WITH CAREER CHOICES

One of the most critical yet often overlooked aspects of achieving workplace success is aligning your personal values with your career choices.

When your values and professional path harmonize, you are more likely to experience satisfaction, motivation, and long-term success.

- **Understanding Personal Values**

Personal values are the core principles that guide your decisions, define your priorities, and shape how you live your life.

Examples include honesty, creativity, collaboration, and work-life balance. These values influence not only your personal life but also your career aspirations and workplace habits.

- **The Importance of Alignment**

When your career aligns with your values, work becomes more than a task—it becomes purposeful. For instance:

- **Fulfillment:** If helping others is a core value, a role in healthcare, education, or social services may bring more satisfaction than one focused purely on financial gain.

- **Motivation:** Working in a field that resonates with your values reduces burnout and increases drive, as you are naturally more engaged in tasks that reflect what matters to you.

- **Growth:** Alignment fosters personal and professional development. You are more likely to excel when you work in an environment that supports your principles.

- **Identifying Your Core Values**

To match your career with your values, start by identifying what truly matters to you. Ask yourself:

1. What activities or achievements make me feel proud or energized?

2. What traits do I admire in others, and how do I embody them?

3. What would I stand firm on, even in challenging situations?

- **Evaluating Career Options**

Once you've identified your values, assess potential careers or roles. Research industries, companies, or roles that prioritize similar principles. Key steps include:

- **Job Descriptions:** Look for phrases that reflect your values, such as "team collaboration" for those who value teamwork or "creative problem-solving" for those who prioritize innovation.

- **Company Culture:** Explore company websites, mission statements, and employee reviews.

Organizations often highlight their guiding principles, which can indicate whether they align with your own.

- **Creating a Value-Driven Work Plan**

If you're already in a job, align your tasks and goals with your values to enhance satisfaction. For example:

- **Autonomy:** If independence is crucial, find ways to take ownership of projects.

- **Impact:** If making a difference matters, identify how your work contributes to broader company goals or societal needs.

If you find misalignment between your career and values, consider gradual shifts, such as requesting new responsibilities, exploring lateral moves, or pursuing further education in a field that better matches your ideals.

- **Benefits of Value Alignment**

When personal values and career choices align, the results are transformative. Employees report higher job satisfaction, increased productivity, and a greater sense of well-being.

Additionally, organizations benefit from value-aligned employees who are more engaged, creative, and committed to their roles.

Matching personal values with career choices is a powerful strategy for workplace success.

It ensures that your professional life not only meets external expectations but also reflects your inner principles.

SIMPLIFYING COMPLEX GOALS INTO MANAGEABLE CHUNKS

When tackling ambitious objectives, the key to progress often lies in breaking them down into smaller, actionable tasks.

In the workplace, this approach is essential for transforming overwhelming goals into achievable milestones.

Simplifying complex goals not only fosters clarity but also boosts confidence and productivity, creating a path toward consistent success.

- **The Power of Breaking It Down**

Complex goals often feel insurmountable when viewed as a whole. However, by dividing them into smaller tasks, you can transform them into a series of straightforward steps.

This process enables you to focus on one task at a time, reducing stress and improving your ability to concentrate.

For example, instead of aiming to "launch a product," you can break it down into tasks like researching market trends, designing prototypes, and creating marketing materials.

Each task becomes an achievable win, building momentum toward the final objective.

- **Prioritization for Clarity**

Once a goal is divided into chunks, prioritizing tasks ensures you focus on what matters most.

Utilize tools like task lists, project boards, or progress charts to organize your steps. Assign deadlines to each task, keeping your progress aligned with overarching timelines.

This method eliminates guesswork and provides a clear roadmap, making even the most complex goals feel attainable.

- **Building Confidence Through Action**

Small wins fuel motivation. Every time you complete a step, you build confidence and reinforce the belief that your larger goal is within reach.

For instance, if your goal is to improve team collaboration, start with manageable steps like scheduling regular team check-ins or creating a shared communication platform.

These actions might seem minor, but their cumulative impact can lead to significant change.

- **Overcoming Procrastination**

Breaking goals into smaller parts also combats procrastination. When tasks feel too big or undefined, it's easy to delay action.

Smaller tasks, however, feel less daunting and encourage immediate engagement.

For example, if writing a report seems overwhelming, start by drafting the outline. This initial step paves the way for subsequent progress, making the task less intimidating.

- **Celebrating Milestones**

Recognizing and celebrating milestones is a crucial aspect of simplifying goals.

Each milestone achieved represents tangible progress and reminds you of how far you've come.

Whether it's completing the first draft of a presentation or reaching a sales target, taking the time to acknowledge your efforts motivates continued success.

- **A Culture of Progress**

Incorporating this habit into workplace routines fosters a culture of progress. Teams can adopt this strategy by breaking projects into phases, assigning clear responsibilities, and maintaining regular check-ins to track progress.

This approach not only keeps everyone aligned but also ensures that challenges are addressed before they escalate.

- **Practical Tips for Simplifying Goals**

1. Define Your Goal Clearly: Write down your goal in specific, measurable terms.

2. Divide and Conquer: Break the goal into smaller tasks or phases.

3. Prioritize Tasks: Identify which steps are most critical and address them first.

4. Set Realistic Deadlines: Assign deadlines that are challenging yet achievable.

5. Track Progress: Use visual tools like charts or apps to monitor your advancement.

6. Celebrate Successes: Reward yourself or your team for achieving key milestones.

CHAPTER

2

MASTERING TIME MANAGEMENT

Are you constantly feeling overwhelmed by your workload? Do you find yourself running out of time for the tasks that matter most? The secret to workplace success isn't working harder—it's mastering time management.

In the fast-paced environment of modern workplaces, effective time management can set you apart as a high performer.

By adopting habits that prioritize what truly matters, minimize distractions, and boost efficiency, you can take control of your day and excel in your role.

This article will guide you through simple yet powerful strategies to maximize productivity without burning out.

Whether it's learning to prioritize tasks, using time-blocking techniques, or knowing when to delegate, these habits are designed to empower you and transform how you approach your workday.

Don't just manage your time—master it. Dive into these practical tips and discover how you can achieve more with less stress.

Get ready to unlock your full potential and create a work-life balance that inspires success.

The workplace values time as a key resource, emphasizing the importance of productivity and efficient use. Mastering time management is essential for achieving productivity, reducing stress, and excelling in your career.

By developing empowering habits, you can take control of your day and optimize your work performance.

1. Prioritize Tasks with a Clear System
To manage time effectively, it's essential to recognize and address the most important tasks and responsibilities.

Use a priority matrix or a simple system to classify tasks into categories like urgent, important, and non-essential.

Focus your energy on the tasks that align with your goals and deadlines. By addressing the most impactful work first, you ensure progress on key objectives.

2. Set Realistic Goals

Break your workload into manageable goals. Create a structured plan to outline and achieve your daily, weekly, and monthly objectives, ensuring focused productivity and progress.

Setting measurable and attainable targets helps you stay focused and motivated, while also avoiding overcommitment.

3. Eliminate Distractions

Distractions can derail even the best-laid plans. Identify the common interruptions in your work environment, such as excessive notifications or non-essential meetings, and implement strategies to minimize them.

Consider creating designated "focus time" during which you can work without interruption.

4. Time scheduling for Efficiency

Time scheduling is an effective technique for managing your schedule. Dedicate specific time slots for each task or project.

As a result, you'll be able to manage your time wisely and avoid putting tasks off until later. By visually seeing your day organized, you gain clarity on where your time goes and how to optimize it.

5. Learn to Say No

Overcommitting can lead to burnout and reduced productivity. Politely declining additional tasks or delegating responsibilities ensures that you can maintain focus on your priorities.

Knowing your limits and communicating them effectively is a skill that will serve you well in any workplace.

6. Regularly Review and Reflect

Schedule daily or weekly check-ins with yourself to evaluate what you've achieved and adjust your strategy as needed.

Conduct a self-assessment of your time management tactics, distinguishing between effective and ineffective methods. Adjust your approach as needed to refine your system and improve continuously.

7. Leverage Tools for Productivity
Utilize practical tools that help you stay organized. Whether it's digital planners, task management apps, or traditional methods like handwritten lists, find what works for you.

These tools should complement your workflow and make tracking progress easier.

PRIORITIZATION TECHNIQUES FOR PEAK PRODUCTIVITY

How can I stay productive when everything on my to-do list feels equally important and overwhelming?

Prioritizing tasks efficiently is the secret to maintaining high productivity levels. Techniques like the Value Matrix Method help you identify what's truly critical versus what can wait, while strategies such as Task scheduling and Goal-Driven Prioritization ensure your focus remains on high-impact tasks.

By aligning your efforts with your energy levels and long-term objectives, you can cut through the noise, avoid burnout, and consistently tackle your most meaningful work.

Discover how to take control of your day and make every moment count with these proven methods.

In the modern workplace, staying productive requires mastering the art of prioritization.

With tasks constantly competing for attention, effective prioritization ensures you focus on what truly matters, driving success and reducing stress.

Improve your workplace productivity and results with these evidence-based prioritization techniques.

1. The Value Matrix Method
Adapted from popular quadrant systems, this technique involves categorizing tasks based on urgency and importance. Create a simple grid with four sections:

- Critical and Immediate: High-priority tasks needing immediate attention.

- Critical but Not Immediate: Important tasks that require planning and scheduling.

- Non-Critical but Immediate: Tasks that are less important but time-sensitive. Delegate these if possible.

- **Non-Critical and Not Immediate:** Low-priority tasks. Consider eliminating or postponing them.

This system allows you to filter through distractions and focus on high-impact work.

2. Goal-Driven Prioritization

Align your tasks with broader goals or objectives. Prioritize tasks by asking, 'Does this align with my key goals?' Direct your attention to activities that create lasting value and drive significant growth.

This approach prevents wasting time on low-value activities and helps maintain a strategic focus.

3. Time scheduling

This approach breaks down your workday into manageable chunks, with set times designated for specific tasks and responsibilities.

Start by scheduling your most demanding tasks during your peak energy hours and leave less demanding activities for later.

Tools like digital calendars or a simple journal can help you visualize and stick to your schedule, minimizing distractions.

4. The Two-Minute Rule

For tasks needing two minutes or less, take action right away. This easy-to-follow guideline keeps small tasks from building up and distracting your mind.

For larger tasks, break them into smaller, actionable steps that can be tackled more easily.

5. Daily Prioritization Lists

Start your day by creating a task list, then rank each item according to its priority. Employ a versatile method, including

- **Must-Do Tasks:** Critical items that must be completed.

- **Should-Do Tasks:** Important but not immediately pressing tasks.

- **Nice-to-Do Tasks:** Low-priority tasks that can be done if time allows.

Revisit this list throughout the day to adjust as needed based on changing priorities.

6. Batching Similar Tasks

Group similar tasks together to maximize efficiency. For instance, dedicate a specific block of time to handle all emails, another for administrative tasks, and another for creative work.

This reduces the mental effort of switching between unrelated tasks, boosting productivity.

7. The One-Thing Principle

Choose one task that, if completed, will make the biggest impact on your day.

Dedicate your attention to completing this task before transitioning to others. This technique keeps you grounded and ensures you tackle your most significant work without feeling overwhelmed.

8. Energy and Focus Prioritization

Sync your tasks with your energy levels to optimize productivity.

Reserve high-energy times for tasks that require deep focus or creativity and lower-energy periods for administrative or repetitive work. This approach optimizes both energy and output.

MANAGING DISTRACTIONS AND STAYING Focused

Picture yourself as a lion prowling the workplace jungle. Your desk is your territory, and your tasks are the prey you must hunt to survive and thrive.

But distractions—like buzzing bees of notifications, sneaky hyenas of small talk, and the swirling fog of clutter—are always circling, trying to pull you away from your focus.

Now, here's the challenge: Will you let the hyenas steal your meal? Will you let the fog blind you from your target? Or will you step into your role as the king or queen of your domain, sharpen your focus, and claim what's yours?

The key to winning in this wild jungle lies in mastering your instincts and tools. You need strategies—your claws and teeth—to swat away the buzzing bees, outwit the sneaky hyenas, and clear the fog.

With empowering habits like creating a distraction-free zone, setting boundaries, and practicing deep work, you'll not only survive but thrive in the jungle, emerging as the leader everyone admires.

Are you ready to assert your authority and become the master of your professional domain? Dive into the strategies that will help you turn distractions into mere background noise and make every day a victory lap. Seize opportunities for success and bask in the glory of your achievements!

Minimizing distractions is crucial to maximizing productivity in contemporary work settings. Whether it's the constant ping of messages, the lure of social media, or an overwhelming to-do list, staying focused has become a challenge.

Building empowering habits to manage distractions can help you reclaim your focus, boost your efficiency, and create a thriving work environment.

1. Understand Your Triggers

Start by identifying what pulls your attention away. Is it notifications, colleagues dropping by, or even your wandering mind? By acknowledging the sources of your distractions, you can craft personalized strategies to stay focused and productive. For instance:

- Turn off non-essential notifications during work hours.

- Set clear boundaries with colleagues, letting them know when you're not available for interruptions.

- Use mindfulness techniques to manage internal distractions, such as deep breathing or quick mental resets.

2. Create a Distraction-Free Zone

Design a workspace that encourages focus. Keep your desk organized, minimize visual clutter, and make it a space where your mind can concentrate on tasks. Digital distractions can also be managed:

- Use tools that block non-work-related websites during your focus hours.

- Keep your phone out of reach or on silent when possible.

3. Prioritize Tasks Using a Focus Framework

Adopt a task management system to keep your priorities in check. Frameworks like the Important-Urgent Matrix or simple daily to-do lists can provide clarity. Start your day by identifying:

- High-priority tasks that demand immediate attention.

- Non-urgent tasks that require focus but can be scheduled.

Prioritizing critical tasks ensures that you make meaningful headway, even if distractions arise later.

4. Adopt the Two-Minute Rule
Small tasks can be distracting if they pile up. The Two-Minute Rule advises completing tasks promptly if their duration is two minutes or less.

This habit prevents minor distractions from lingering in your mind, freeing up mental space for larger tasks.

5. Leverage the Power of Deep Work

Deep work involves dedicating uninterrupted time and attention to tackling intellectually demanding tasks. To cultivate this habit:

- Make time for intense, undivided attention on critical tasks every day.

- Share your focused work schedule with others to protect your productivity and minimize interruptions.

- Pair deep work sessions with an end-of-session review to track progress.

BUILDING CONSISTENT DAILY ROUTINES

Success is not built in a day but in the disciplined rhythm of daily habits; the consistency of small, intentional actions is the quiet force that transforms fleeting potential into lasting excellence.

Success in the workplace isn't accidental—it's the result of intentional actions, practiced daily, to align productivity with personal and professional goals.

Building consistent daily routines not only fosters discipline but also creates a framework for achieving sustained workplace success.

Here's how you can design and stick to empowering habits for a thriving career.

- **Start with a Clear Morning Routine**

The way you begin your day lays the foundation for achievement or struggle. A purposeful morning routine can help you transition smoothly into a productive mindset.

Instead of reaching for your phone or rushing out the door, try:

- **Mindful preparation:** Spend a few minutes practicing gratitude, setting daily intentions, or meditating to center your thoughts.

- **Physical activity:** Even a short stretch or brisk walk can invigorate your body and mind, enhancing focus and reducing stress.

- **Planning your day:** Use a notebook or digital planner to outline key priorities, tasks, and goals. This helps ensure you start your day with direction.

- **Structure Your Work Hours for Productivity**

Workplace success often hinges on your ability to manage time effectively. To build a productive routine, try these strategies:

- **Time blocking:** Assign fixed hours to essential tasks to ensure concentrated effort. For example, assign your most challenging or creative work to the hours when your energy and focus are at their peak.

- **Breaks:** Incorporate short breaks to avoid burnout. The "focus-rest-focus" pattern is highly effective in maintaining long-term productivity.

- **Minimize distractions:** Turn off nonessential notifications and set boundaries for when and how you engage with interruptions, such as emails or unplanned meetings.

- **Emphasize Consistency Over Perfection**

The goal is not to create a rigid or perfect routine but one that works for you and evolves with your needs.

Maintaining a steady pace helps form enduring habits and generates unstoppable momentum.

- **Adaptability:** Life and work demands fluctuate, so allow room to adjust your routine without guilt.

- **Reflection:** Spend time at the end of each day assessing what worked well and what needs improvement. Adjust your routine as necessary to maintain alignment with your goals.

- **Incorporate Self-Care into Your Routine**

Disregarding self-care needs can lead to diminished performance, chronic fatigue, and burnout. A successful routine isn't just about work; it's about creating a balanced life.

- **Physical health:** Incorporate nutritious meals, regular exercise, and sufficient hydration.

- **Mental health:** Dedicate time to unwind, whether through reading, hobbies, or quality time with loved ones.

- **Sleep:** Prioritize consistent sleep patterns to enhance focus and cognitive performance.

End the Day with Purpose

A solid evening routine is just as crucial as a strong morning. Winding down intentionally prepares your mind for rest and your body for recovery.

- **Review your day:** Assess your progress, celebrate wins and learn from obstacles. Note areas for improvement or tasks to carry forward.

- **Prepare for tomorrow:** Organize your workspace, set goals, and plan a to-do list for the next day.

- **Relaxation:** Engage in activities that help you relax, such as light reading or listening to calming music.

- **Small Steps, Big Impact**

Creating lasting daily routines takes time, effort, and a commitment to steady progress. Start small—implement one new habit at a time and build gradually.

Celebrate your progress, no matter how small, and remember that every positive change contributes to a more empowered and successful work life.

CHAPTER

3

BUILDING EFFECTIVE COMMUNICATION SKILLS

James, a newly promoted team leader at a bustling marketing firm, felt confident about his technical expertise but struggled with communicating effectively.

His team's productivity began to falter, and James couldn't figure out why. One day, during a routine meeting, he noticed a quiet team member, Sarah, trying to share her idea.

Her voice was drowned out by louder colleagues, and James let it slide—just like he always did.

Later, Sarah hesitantly approached him with the same idea. Her suggestion was brilliant and ultimately turned the project around.

This moment was a turning point for James. He realized that effective communication isn't just about speaking clearly; it's about listening actively, valuing input, and fostering an environment where everyone feels heard.

From that day forward, James made it his mission to improve his communication skills and create a collaborative workplace culture.

This simple yet profound realization underscores the importance of building effective communication habits to succeed in the workplace.

The cornerstone of workplace success isn't merely intelligence or effort; it's the ability to communicate ideas, bridge misunderstandings, and build relationships that thrive on mutual respect.

- **Empowering Habits for Workplace Success**

1. The Art of Listening: Hearing Beyond Words
Active listening is one of the most undervalued yet powerful communication tools.

When you listen attentively, you pick up on the subtle cues that reveal the speaker's emotional state, values, and goals. This helps create trust and promotes responsive, well-considered communication.

Practical Tips:

- Make eye contact to demonstrate your focus and interest.

- Summarize or restate essential information to confirm you're on the same page.

- Avoid distractions—put away your phone and focus entirely on the speaker.

2. Clarity in Expression: Saying What You Mean

Ineffective communication can lead to costly mistakes, wasted effort, and decreased efficiency.

Practice expressing yourself with clarity and precision. Choose words that are simple yet impactful and avoid overloading conversations with unnecessary jargon.

Practical Tips:
- Organize your thoughts before speaking.

- Use examples to explain complex ideas.

- Invite feedback to verify your message resonated as intended.

3. Empathy in Action: Connecting on a Human Level
Empathy is the glue that binds effective communication.

When you approach conversations with empathy, you demonstrate that you value the other person's perspective, even if you disagree. This habit can de-escalate conflicts and build stronger relationships.

Practical Tips:

- Validate others' emotional experiences to create a supportive and non-judgmental space.

- Show understanding and validation by saying 'I appreciate your perspective' or 'That must have been difficult'."

- Show respect and empathy by patiently letting others express themselves completely, without rushing or interrupting.

4. Non-Verbal Communication: Speaking Without Words

Unspoken signals such as body language, facial expressions, and vocal tone can be just as impactful as the words you choose.

Learning to align your non-verbal cues with your verbal messages ensures authenticity and builds trust.

Practical Tips:

- Smile authentically to create a welcoming and positive atmosphere.

- Maintain an open posture by avoiding crossed arms, which can unintentionally convey resistance or guardedness.

- Use subtle mirroring techniques to echo the other person's nonverbal cues, fostering a sense of mutual connection and trust.

5. Mastering Feedback: Giving and Receiving Gracefully

Feedback is crucial for growth, but its potential is often wasted due to inadequate delivery or reception.

Delivering feedback effectively requires balancing honesty with tact, while receiving it demands humility and a willingness to improve.

Practical Tips:
- Target precise behaviors or actions that can be changed, rather than criticizing inherent traits.

- Use a balanced approach to feedback: start and end with positive reinforcement, and insert actionable suggestions for improvement.

- Demonstrate a growth mindset by listening attentively to feedback, allowing the speaker to finish, and acknowledging their contribution.

Effective communication isn't a one-time skill to master—it's a lifelong habit to refine.

ACTIVE LISTENING FOR BETTER UNDERSTANDING

True success in the workplace is not found in speaking louder, but in listening deeper. When you embrace the art of active listening, you unlock understanding, dissolve barriers, and cultivate trust.

Through this, conversations transform into connections, conflicts give way to solutions, and ordinary interactions become the foundation for extraordinary achievements.

The power to lead, innovate, and inspire begins with the simple act of truly hearing others.

In the fast-paced environment of today's workplace, effective communication is a cornerstone of success.

At the heart of exceptional communication lies **active listening**, an empowering habit that can transform professional relationships, enhance collaboration, and pave the way for workplace success.

- **What is Active Listening?**

Active listening is a multifaceted process that involves attentive engagement, comprehension of the speaker's perspective, and a considered reply.

This habit lays the groundwork for trustworthy relationships, clear communication, and constructive dialogue. When practiced consistently, it becomes a vital tool for personal and professional growth.

- **Key Elements of Active Listening**

To develop this skill, focus on the following components:

1. Giving Full Attention

Set aside distractions such as phones, emails, or unrelated thoughts. Use body language, such as nodding or maintaining eye contact, to show that you are present and engaged.

2. Clarifying and Paraphrasing

Ask open-ended questions or rephrase the speaker's points to confirm your understanding.

For example, you might say, "If I understand correctly, you're suggesting..." This step ensures mutual clarity.

3. Acknowledging Nonverbal Cues

Pick up on the speaker's subtle cues, such as tone, facial expressions, and body language, to better comprehend their intended meaning. These cues often provide deeper insight into their message or emotions.

4. Providing Constructive Feedback

Rather than reacting impulsively, take a brief moment to collect your thoughts and respond more mindfully. Offer feedback that shows you value their perspective, even if you disagree. For instance, "Your insight is helpful. Would you mind explaining further so we can fully comprehend the idea?

5. Avoiding Interruptions

Let the speaker complete their thoughts before offering input. This strategy cultivates a trusting environment, leading to more authentic and candid conversations.

- **Positive Outcomes of Mindful Communication at Work**

When embraced as a habit, active listening leads to:

- **Improved Team Collaboration**: Teams that practice active listening experience fewer conflicts and achieve greater alignment on goals.

- **Enhanced Problem-Solving:** Understanding different perspectives enables innovative solutions to challenges.

- **Stronger Relationships:** Genuine listening fosters trust and mutual respect among colleagues.

- **Personal Development:** Active listening enhances emotional intelligence, a skill highly valued in leadership roles.

- **Tips for Building Active Listening Skills**

1. Practice Mindfulness: Train yourself to stay present in conversations. When distractions arise, softly steer your attention back to the speaker to ensure you're fully present and engaged.

2. Create Safe Spaces: Foster an environment where colleagues feel comfortable expressing their ideas.

3. Seek Feedback: Ask trusted coworkers how you can improve your listening habits.

4. Set Personal Goals: Commit to practicing active listening in at least one conversation each day.

Active listening is not just a workplace skill—it's a habit that empowers individuals to connect, collaborate, and lead more effectively.

SPEAKING WITH CLARITY AND CONFIDENCE

True clarity in communication is not just about the words you speak but the conviction behind them.

Confidence is born from preparation, strengthened by authenticity, and elevated through understanding.

When you master the art of clear and confident expression, you do more than share ideas—you inspire trust, foster connection, and pave the path to lasting success in every interaction.

Clarity and confidence in communication are foundational habits for thriving in any professional environment.

When you articulate your ideas clearly and with assurance, you establish yourself as a credible and trustworthy team member, paving the way for career growth.

Here are some actionable strategies to enhance your speaking abilities and empower your workplace interactions.

1. Understand Your Message
Before you speak, ensure you fully comprehend the message you want to convey. Ask yourself:

- What is the purpose of my message?

- Who is my audience?

- What outcome am I seeking?

Having a clear goal prevents rambling and helps your audience grasp the core of your communication.

2. Structure Your Thoughts
Organize your ideas logically. Use a framework like:
- **Introduction:** Briefly state your main point.

- **Body:** Present supporting details or arguments.

- **Conclusion:** Summarize and emphasize the takeaway.

This structure keeps your communication concise and focused, especially in meetings or presentations.

3. Cultivate a Strong, Clear Voice

The tone and clarity of your voice can significantly impact how your message is received. Practice these techniques:

- **Enunciation:** Speak distinctly to ensure every word is heard.

- **Pace:** Avoid speaking too fast or too slow; find a comfortable rhythm.

- **Volume:** Speak loudly enough to be heard but not so loud as to overpower.

Record yourself or practice with a colleague to identify areas for improvement.

4. Expand Your Vocabulary

Having a rich vocabulary enables you to express ideas with precision.

However, avoid using overly complex words that may confuse your audience. Strive for language that is professional yet relatable.

5. Adopt Positive Body Language

Non-verbal cues, such as maintaining eye contact, using open gestures, and standing with good posture, reinforce your spoken words.

Confidence is as much about how you present yourself as it is about what you say.

6. Prepare and Practice

Preparation breeds confidence. For important conversations, presentations, or meetings:

- Draft an outline of your key points.

- Rehearse in front of a mirror or record yourself to refine delivery.

- Anticipate potential questions and prepare answers.

Repetition builds familiarity and reduces anxiety, helping you speak more fluidly.

8. Embrace Feedback

Constructive criticism is a gift. Request feedback from colleagues or mentors to gain insights into your communication style and identify areas for improvement. Use their insights to fine-tune your approach and identify areas for growth.

NAVIGATING CHALLENGING CONVERSATIONS

Mastering challenging conversations is not about winning an argument but about building bridges where walls once stood.

It is the art of speaking with clarity, listening with empathy, and seeking understanding over dominance.

In these moments, you create not just solutions but connections, fostering a workplace where respect and collaboration transform conflict into progress.

Navigating challenging conversations in the workplace is an essential skill that can significantly influence your professional success.

These discussions often arise when addressing sensitive topics, resolving conflicts, or providing constructive feedback.

While they may seem daunting, mastering this ability can foster trust, collaboration, and mutual respect among colleagues.

One effective approach is to prepare thoroughly before the conversation. Take the time to understand the issue at hand and consider the perspective of the other party.

Clarity is key—determine the core message you want to convey and focus on how it can contribute to a positive outcome.

Begin the dialogue with an open and respectful tone, ensuring that your intentions are clear and devoid of defensiveness.

Active listening is essential to the success of these interactions. Giving the other person space to express their thoughts without interruption demonstrates empathy and builds rapport.

Paraphrasing their points can affirm that you value their input, creating a foundation for productive discussion.

This approach also allows for mutual understanding, helping to de-escalate potential tension.

Maintaining composure is vital, particularly in emotionally charged scenarios. Practicing emotional intelligence—staying aware of your own emotions while managing your reactions—can prevent the conversation from becoming confrontational.

A calm demeanor encourages the other party to reciprocate, fostering a constructive environment where solutions can emerge.

Using neutral and inclusive language further ensures that the dialogue remains professional.

Avoid accusatory statements or overly technical jargon that could alienate the other party.

Instead, frame your concerns collaboratively, emphasizing shared goals and outcomes. This approach not only mitigates defensiveness but also promotes a sense of teamwork.

Concluding the conversation with clear next steps or agreements can reinforce the progress made.

Summarize key points discussed and confirm mutual understanding to ensure alignment moving forward.

Whether the resolution involves actionable steps or a commitment to revisit the topic, a clear closure signals professionalism and respect.

Navigating these interactions effectively requires practice and patience. As you develop this habit, you'll find that your ability to handle difficult conversations contributes to your overall workplace success.

It demonstrates your commitment to fostering positive relationships and building an environment where collaboration thrives.

CHAPTER

4

DEVELOPING A GROWTH MINDSET

History offers countless lessons about the power of persistence and adaptability.

Consider the story of the pioneering nurse and healthcare reformer, renowned for establishing modern nursing standards.

Born into a privileged family in the 19th century, she faced immense societal pressure to conform to the roles of women in her time.

Yet, she pursued her passion for healthcare, often working in dire conditions.

What set her apart wasn't just her skill but her mindset—a relentless belief in growth and her ability to inspire transformative habits within her field.

Her story echoes the truth that lasting success comes not from static talents but from cultivating empowering behaviors that drive continuous improvement.

In today's workplace, this principle holds strong. Whether you're navigating corporate hierarchies, leading a team, or building your career from the ground up, the habits you develop and the mindset you embrace directly influence your trajectory.

The good news is that anyone can learn to cultivate habits that lead to empowerment and success.

The contemporary workplace has evolved substantially, distinguishing it from previous generations. The accelerating rate of digital transformation necessitates a culture of continuous learning, innovation, and flexibility within individuals and organizations.

If you feel stuck, overwhelmed, or unsure about how to thrive in such an environment, you're not alone. Many professionals face the same challenges.

But what if the key to thriving isn't about working harder or longer hours? What if it's about working differently—by focusing on developing habits that empower you to grow and excel?

Imagine a colleague who seems to flourish in any situation, embracing challenges with enthusiasm and learning from failures without fear.

What separates them from others isn't a higher IQ or luck—it's their approach to growth.

This book is your guide to unlocking those same principles, helping you embrace habits that make you more resilient, adaptable, and effective in the workplace.

A growth mindset is the foundation of empowering habits. Coined to describe the belief that abilities can be developed through effort, learning, and persistence, this mindset shifts the focus from fixed limitations to boundless potential.

When paired with actionable habits, it becomes the engine that drives workplace success.

Begin developing a growth mindset by redefining difficulties as opportunities to learn, adapt, and evolve. For instance, when faced with a project outside your expertise, see it as a chance to learn and expand your skills rather than as an obstacle.

Replace self-doubt with curiosity, asking yourself, "What can I gain from this experience?" This minor shift in perspective has a profound impact, reducing stress and unlocking the potential for creative and innovative solutions.

Empowering habits also play a critical role. Cultivate habits that reinforce your belief in progress.

Start with reflection: set aside time each week to evaluate your achievements, challenges, and lessons learned.

Next, build habits around learning, such as dedicating 20 minutes daily to reading or practicing a skill relevant to your role.

Over time, these practices compound, boosting both your confidence and competence.

Equally important is fostering collaboration. A growth mindset thrives in environments where ideas are exchanged, and feedback is welcomed.

Build relationships with colleagues who inspire you and engage in constructive conversations that push you to think beyond your current limitations.

Remember that mistakes are an essential part of the learning process, leading to personal and professional growth.

Adopting habits that embrace resilience—like journaling your progress or discussing setbacks with a mentor—keeps you moving forward with clarity and purpose.

The story of workplace success is not written in moments of perfection but in the steady habits that empower individuals to grow, adapt, and thrive.

EMBRACING CHALLENGES AS OPPORTUNITIES

In the late 1800s, during the height of industrial expansion, a young man named George found himself laboring in a factory under grueling conditions. With no formal education and limited resources, he faced insurmountable odds.

Despite the daily grind, George chose to approach every challenge with determination, learning from setbacks and observing how machinery worked.

Over time, his persistence paid off—he designed a process that revolutionized the industry, eventually founding one of the most successful enterprises of his time.

George's story is a testament to how challenges, when embraced with the right mindset, can be stepping stones to greatness.

This historical narrative underscores a universal truth: challenges are not roadblocks but pathways to growth. It is not the absence of hardship but the way we face it that defines our success.

Picture yourself in the workplace, where deadlines loom, interpersonal conflicts arise, and unexpected projects disrupt your plans.

These moments are more than just stressors—they are opportunities waiting to be seized.

Imagine harnessing the energy from these difficulties to refine your skills, build stronger relationships, and showcase resilience.

When approached with intentionality and the right habits, challenges can become catalysts for professional and personal success.

In a world where the workplace is constantly evolving, the ability to transform obstacles into opportunities is a game-changer.

This outlook boosts your performance and showcases your ability to lead effectively, even in challenging circumstances.

It's about adopting empowering habits that reshape how you perceive and respond to difficulties, turning every setback into a springboard for success.

Workplace challenges are inevitable, but your response to them can define your trajectory.

Empowering habits, such as cultivating a growth mindset, seeking creative solutions, and maintaining composure, are vital tools for success.

A growth mindset allows you to transform setbacks into learning experiences, fueling personal and professional growth. For instance, when a project fails, instead of succumbing to frustration, analyze what went wrong, identify areas for improvement, and apply those insights to future tasks.

Similarly, fostering collaboration can transform challenges into opportunities for innovation.

When faced with a problem, engaging with colleagues and pooling diverse ideas can lead to breakthroughs that might not have been possible in isolation.

These habits not only solve immediate problems but also build a culture of resilience and adaptability.

Keeping a level head under pressure is a distinguishing characteristic of high-achieving professionals. Stressful situations are inevitable, but how you manage them sets you apart.

By practicing mindfulness and emotional intelligence, you can navigate high-pressure environments with clarity and confidence, inspiring those around you to do the same.

When challenges arise, view them as opportunities to refine your skills, strengthen your team, and demonstrate your capacity for growth.

By embracing this mindset and building empowering habits, you pave the way for sustained success in any workplace.

The next time a challenge comes your way, remember: within every obstacle lies the seed of an opportunity waiting to be realized.

LEARNING FROM FEEDBACK AND MISTAKES

In 1879, after countless experiments, a renowned American inventor famously remarked, "I have not failed. My experimentation has revealed 10,000 unsuccessful solutions."

This iconic statement is more than just an anecdote; it captures the essence of turning mistakes into stepping stones.

This pioneering innovator's perseverance didn't just light up rooms—it illuminated the potential for personal and professional success when one embraces the lessons hidden within setbacks.

In today's dynamic workplace, learning from feedback and mistakes is not merely an option; it is an essential habit for success.

Feedback, whether it feels constructive or critical, is a mirror reflecting areas for growth.

Mistakes, on the other hand, are opportunities in disguise—if approached with the right mindset.

The habit of seeking out and embracing feedback can transform a stagnant career into a flourishing one, just as reflecting on mistakes can spark innovation and resilience.

By creating a culture of self-awareness, professionals empower themselves to rise above challenges.

They understand that feedback is not an attack but a gift, offering insights that may not be immediately obvious.

The most empowered individuals actively seek out opportunities to refine their skills, viewing each critique as a compass pointing toward success.

Imagine the workplace as a stage, with each individual performing a unique role.

Now picture an orchestra where every musician learns not only from their own notes but also from the harmonies and dissonances around them.

This is what feedback and mistakes represent in a professional setting. Reflection is the act of stopping to listen to these harmonies—of assessing where things might have gone awry and envisioning how they could align better.

To engage deeply with this practice, individuals must first let go of defensiveness. Accepting feedback requires courage, especially when it feels personal.

Yet, this very act of vulnerability becomes the seed for growth. When employees reflect on their errors, not as evidence of incompetence but as raw material for mastery, they gain an edge that sets them apart.

This habit is contagious. Teams that foster open conversations around feedback and mistakes without fear of judgment create a culture where everyone grows together.

Such environments become places of innovation, creativity, and trust. Employees feel empowered to experiment and learn, knowing that mistakes are not the end but rather the beginning of something better.

The workplace is not free of obstacles—it never has been, nor will it ever be. But what distinguishes successful individuals is their perspective.

Challenges are not walls that block progress; they are mountains that call out to be climbed. Every difficult situation holds the potential for growth and transformation.

When you approach challenges as opportunities, you shift the narrative. An overwhelming project becomes a chance to hone leadership skills.

A strained relationship with a colleague becomes an invitation to develop emotional intelligence.

This perspective doesn't just help you overcome hurdles—it transforms those hurdles into the very tools that strengthen your professional capabilities.

Consider a challenging moment in your career as a seed waiting to sprout. It might require patience, nurturing, and perhaps a little rain, but with persistence, it will bloom.

By embracing this mindset, you cultivate resilience, adaptability, and confidence—traits that define empowered professionals.

Moreover, your ability to navigate challenges inspires others, turning you into a beacon of positivity and resourcefulness within your workplace.

Learning from feedback and mistakes, reflecting deeply on them, and embracing challenges as opportunities are not isolated habits.

Together, they create a symphony of empowerment. Each habit feeds into the next, forming a cycle of continuous improvement.

Those who embody these habits thrive not only as professionals but as leaders who uplift others.

Empowering habits like these transform ordinary workdays into opportunities for growth and innovation.

CULTIVATING RESILIENCE IN THE WORKPLACE

Resilience in the workplace isn't about avoiding challenges—it's about transforming them into opportunities, fueled by self-awareness, a growth mindset, and the strength of community.

When we cultivate empowering habits, we don't just survive the pressures of work; we rise above them, creating a culture of adaptability, innovation, and enduring success.

Cultivating resilience in the workplace is a cornerstone of professional success.

In today's dynamic environment, the ability to adapt, persevere, and thrive under pressure distinguishes top performers and creates a positive, productive work culture.

By adopting empowering habits, individuals and teams can foster a resilient mindset, paving the way for sustainable success.

Resilience begins with self-awareness. Understanding personal strengths and stressors helps individuals navigate challenges effectively.

This awareness can be developed through reflective practices, such as journaling or mindfulness exercises, which promote clarity and emotional balance.

When employees are in tune with their emotions and reactions, they can make intentional decisions rather than reactive ones, even during high-pressure situations.

Another crucial aspect of resilience is maintaining a growth mindset. This approach sees setbacks not as debilitating failures, but as stepping stones for education and improvement.

Embracing curiosity and a willingness to experiment fosters an environment where mistakes are not feared but rather valued as part of the process.

This habit encourages innovation and continuous improvement, vital traits in any competitive workplace.

Building supportive relationships also strengthens workplace resilience. Collaboration and mutual trust among colleagues create a safety net that helps employees bounce back from challenges more effectively.

Sharing experiences, seeking advice, and offering encouragement promote a sense of community and shared purpose.

When employees feel supported, their capacity to handle stress and adapt to change increases significantly.

Healthy habits are equally critical for resilience. Prioritizing physical health through regular exercise, balanced nutrition, and sufficient sleep enhances energy levels and mental clarity.

Emotional resilience can be bolstered by setting boundaries, ensuring work-life balance, and engaging in activities that bring joy and relaxation outside of work.

These practices ensure employees remain focused, energized, and ready to tackle challenges.

Resilient individuals also practice proactive stress management. Techniques such as deep breathing, meditation, or progressive relaxation help to manage stress in real-time, preventing it from escalating into burnout.

Employers can further empower their teams by fostering a culture that normalizes conversations about stress and mental well-being, providing access to resources and support when needed.

Finally, clear communication and goal setting empower employees to stay aligned and motivated.

When objectives are transparent and achievable, teams work cohesively and can better navigate obstacles together.

Regular feedback and recognition of achievements reinforce resilience by reminding employees of their value and progress.

CHAPTER

5

FOSTERING COLLABORATION AND TEAMWORK

True workplace success is not built on individual achievements but on the collective strength of a united team—where open communication fuels innovation, trust binds every member, and diverse perspectives shape extraordinary outcomes.

Collaboration isn't just a skill; it's the heartbeat of progress and the bridge to limitless potential.

Successful organizations in the contemporary work landscape rely heavily on the power of collaboration and teamwork to drive innovation, productivity, and growth.

A well-coordinated team can achieve remarkable results, blending diverse skills and perspectives into a cohesive effort.

But fostering a culture of collaboration doesn't happen by chance—it requires deliberate actions, shared values, and empowering habits that set the stage for a united and productive environment.

1. Emphasizing Open Communication

Clear and open communication is the bedrock of effective teamwork. Encouraging team members to share ideas, ask questions, and provide feedback creates an atmosphere of trust and mutual respect.

Leaders can promote this by organizing regular team check-ins, maintaining transparency about goals, and actively listening to the concerns and suggestions of their team.

When everyone feels heard, they are more likely to engage and contribute meaningfully.

2. Cultivating a Shared Vision

A shared vision provides a clear direction and focus, aligning individual efforts with organizational goals. This alignment fosters a sense of purpose and helps individuals see how their contributions fit into the larger picture.

Leaders can establish this by clearly defining goals and involving the team in the planning process.

Shared ownership of the vision enables effortless collaboration, as team members work together to achieve a mutually desired outcome.

3. Encouraging Diverse Perspectives

Diversity of thought fuels innovation. Team members' individual strengths, experiences, and insights come together to create a vibrant and dynamic team culture.

Encouraging the expression of different perspectives enriches problem-solving and strengthens decision-making.

This can be achieved by creating an inclusive culture where every voice is valued and where differing opinions are seen as opportunities rather than obstacles.

4. Building Trust Through Accountability

Trust serves as the unifying force that strengthens team relationships and promotes effective teamwork. One of the most effective ways to build trust is by fostering a culture of accountability.

This means ensuring that everyone, including leaders, fulfills their commitments and takes responsibility for their actions. When team members trust each other to do their part, collaboration flows more smoothly.

5. Leveraging Individual Strengths

Effective teamwork doesn't mean everyone does the same thing. It means assigning roles that align with individual strengths and interests.

Recognizing the unique abilities of each team member allows them to shine in their areas of expertise, creating a synergy that enhances the team's overall performance.

Leaders can identify these strengths through regular one-on-one discussions and performance reviews.

6. Practicing Empathy and Emotional Intelligence

Collaboration thrives in an environment where empathy is a core value.

Understanding and respecting the feelings, challenges, and motivations of team members fosters stronger bonds and minimizes conflicts.

Leaders who model emotional intelligence—by managing their emotions and responding thoughtfully to others—set the tone for a workplace where collaboration can flourish.

7. Providing Opportunities for Skill Development

Investing in team members' growth boosts morale and equips them with the tools needed for effective collaboration.

This can include offering training programs, mentorship opportunities, and resources for learning new skills.

A team that is constantly growing in knowledge and capability is better prepared to tackle challenges together.

8. Celebrating Successes Together

Recognition and celebration are powerful motivators. When a team achieves a milestone, it's important to celebrate together.

Acknowledging contributions, whether through verbal praise, rewards, or team events, reinforces a sense of accomplishment and strengthens the bonds among team members.

9. Addressing Conflicts Constructively

Conflicts are inevitable in any group setting, but how they are handled makes all the difference.

Encouraging a problem-solving approach, rather than blame, ensures that disagreements lead to growth rather than division.

Team members should be empowered to address conflicts openly and respectfully, focusing on solutions that benefit everyone.

BUILDING TRUST WITHIN TEAMS

Imagine a workplace where ideas flow freely, collaboration feels natural, and every team member is genuinely invested in the success of the group. What's the secret ingredient? Trust.

In Empowering Habits for Workplace Success, we reveal how trust isn't just a buzzword but the cornerstone of high-performing teams.

Building trust isn't complicated, but it requires consistent, intentional habits—habits that can transform strained dynamics into thriving connections.

What makes this journey even more powerful is the foundation laid in my previous book, Leading with Trust and Teamwork.

It's here that I unpack the deeper principles of trust and collaboration, offering practical tools for leaders and team members alike.

When paired with the actionable habits in Empowering Habits for Workplace Success, you'll have a roadmap to reshape how your team works together.

Every workplace struggles with the same questions: How do we get everyone on the same page? How can we encourage innovation while staying accountable? And most importantly, how do we build a team that genuinely enjoys working together?

The answer lies in trust. Without it, teams are just groups of individuals working in silos. With it, they become unstoppable forces of creativity and achievement.

This book isn't just about theory; it's about habits you can start today. Whether it's embracing transparency, cultivating respect, or holding yourself accountable, these steps will breathe new life into your workplace culture.

If you're ready to empower your team with trust, don't just stop here. Dive into the habits that make trust tangible in **Empowering Habits for Workplace Success**, and discover the deeper framework in **Leading with Trust and Teamwork.**

Together, these books provide everything you need to turn your workplace into a powerhouse of collaboration and success. Start now—because the strongest teams are built one habit at a time.

A culture of trust is the cornerstone of successful teams in today's fast-moving business landscape. Even the most talented teams can underperform if trust is absent.

But with trust, collaboration becomes seamless, innovation thrives, and challenges transform into opportunities.

In **Empowering Habits for Workplace Success**, we explore practical ways to cultivate trust, offering actionable steps that align with real-world dynamics.

- **Why Trust Matters**

Trust is the thread that weaves team members together, creating a fabric of collaboration and mutual support. When trust is present, employees feel safe to share ideas, give honest feedback, and support one another.

This environment fosters creativity and efficiency, leading to better outcomes for individuals and organizations alike.

- **Habits That Foster Trust**

1. Transparency in Communication

Trust flourishes in environments where communication is open, honest, and free-flowing. Teams thrive when leaders and members share information clearly and consistently, avoiding hidden agendas.

Regular check-ins and open forums for discussion can bridge gaps and nurture understanding.

2. Consistency in Actions

Trust grows when team members follow through on promises. Whether it's meeting deadlines, delivering quality work, or being available to support a colleague, consistency shows reliability and builds respect.

3. Mutual Respect

A team that values each member's contributions creates a foundation of trust. Encouraging diverse perspectives and appreciating each person's unique strengths make people feel valued and secure.

4. Accountability for All

Trust isn't just about leaders; it's about every team member taking responsibility for their actions.

A culture of accountability reinforces the idea that everyone is equally invested in the team's success.

If you're seeking to go beyond habits and dive deeper into building a foundation of trust, my previous book, **Leading with Trust and Teamwork,** provides valuable insights.

In it, I explore the psychology of trust, offer real-world examples, and share leadership strategies that are applicable to any team.

These strategies can complement the habits discussed in Empowering Habits for Workplace Success, providing a holistic approach to transforming your workplace relationships.

Building trust within teams doesn't happen overnight—it's a journey shaped by consistent habits and intentional leadership.

By fostering an environment of transparency, respect, and accountability, you can unlock your team's full potential.

Take the next step by incorporating these empowering habits into your daily work culture.

And for an even deeper understanding, explore the foundational principles in **Leading with Trust and Teamwork.**

Together, these resources can help you transform your workplace into a hub of success and collaboration.

EFFECTIVE DELEGATION AND FEEDBACK

Picture this: A ship sailing on a vibrant sea, its captain standing confidently at the helm.

The crew, a diverse mix of talents and skills, moves seamlessly—some hoisting sails, others navigating the map, and a few ensuring the cargo is secure.

The captain doesn't do it all; instead, they delegate each task to the best-suited crew member, trusting them to deliver.

Occasionally, the captain gathers everyone on deck for a quick chat. "The sails look great, but let's tighten that rigging before the wind shifts," they say, blending encouragement with actionable advice.

The crew nods, energized by the recognition of their work and the clear direction for improvement.

This harmonious scene captures the essence of effective delegation and feedback: the captain empowers the crew, ensuring every hand contributes to the ship's success.

Without this balance, the ship might drift aimlessly or worse, sink under the weight of disorganization.

But with a culture of trust and open communication, the ship sails smoothly toward its destination—just like a thriving workplace.

Ready to become the captain of your own ship and guide your team to success? Dive into the principles of effective delegation and feedback to steer your workplace toward unparalleled achievement.

Effective delegation and feedback are pivotal skills that empower leaders and teams to thrive in dynamic workplace environments.

These habits, when cultivated, create a culture of trust, accountability, and continuous improvement. Here's how to master these essential practices for workplace success.

- **The Art of Delegation**

Delegation goes beyond task assignment; it's about empowering team members to utilize their strengths and contribute to the team's overall goals.

Effective delegation requires a solid understanding of the task objectives, team capabilities, and the outcomes you want to achieve. Here are key principles to enhance your delegation skills:

1. Know Your Team's Strengths

Discover and leverage the diverse skills, interests, and experiences that each team member brings to the table. By aligning tasks with their expertise, you boost efficiency and morale.

2. Define Clear Expectations

Provide a comprehensive outline of the task, including objectives, deadlines, and quality standards. Ambiguity can lead to miscommunication and inefficiencies.

3. Empower, Don't Micromanage

Have confidence in your team's abilities and allow them to approach tasks with their own unique perspective. While guidance is essential, excessive oversight stifles creativity and autonomy.

4. Provide Resources and Support

Empower your team's success by ensuring they have access to relevant training, resources, and information. A well-prepared team is a confident team.

5. Follow Up Without Hovering

Set check-ins at key milestones to assess progress, provide feedback, and address challenges. This ensures accountability while respecting autonomy.

- **Giving Constructive Feedback**

Feedback serves as a catalyst for learning, innovation, and growth, enabling individuals and teams to adapt, improve, and thrive.

When delivered effectively, it enhances performance, builds trust, and fosters a culture of continuous learning. Here's how to provide feedback that empowers:

1. Be Specific and Actionable

Avoid vague statements. Instead of saying, "Good job," specify what was done well, such as, "Your detailed report highlighted key insights that will help guide our strategy."

2. Separate the issue from the individual and provide constructive feedback on the behavior itself

Target the behavior that needs improvement, rather than attacking the person's character. For instance, replace "You're careless" with "There were some oversights in the report that we should review."

3. Balance Positive and Constructive Feedback

Lead with praise and recognition, then address areas that need development. This approach maintains motivation while encouraging growth.

4. Encourage Dialogue

Solicit their feedback and opinions to foster open communication. Collaborative feedback discussions build mutual respect and often lead to creative solutions.

5. Timely Delivery

Deliver feedback soon after the event to facilitate learning and improvement. Delayed feedback loses impact and relevance.

6. End with Encouragement

Conclude feedback sessions with a note of confidence in the individual's ability to improve or sustain their performance.

- **Creating a Feedback-Driven Culture**

Organizations that prioritize feedback create an environment where team members feel valued and motivated. Leaders must model and champion the behaviors and values that define the desired culture.

1. Model Receptive Behavior

Show openness to receiving feedback from peers and subordinates. This reflects a leader's humility and dedication to ongoing learning and self-improvement.

2. Incorporate Regular Feedback Opportunities

Regularly meet with team members to review performance, set goals, and exchange constructive feedback. Consistency reinforces the importance of feedback.

3. Celebrate Successes

Recognize and reward achievements publicly to boost morale and reinforce positive behaviors.

4. Address Challenges Privately

Constructive feedback is best delivered in one-on-one settings to maintain dignity and confidentiality.

COMPASSIONATE CONFLICT MANAGEMENT

Conflict in the workplace is inevitable. Whether it arises from differing opinions, miscommunication, or high-pressure situations, how you handle conflict can significantly impact your professional relationships and overall workplace environment.

Compassionate conflict management is an empowering habit that not only resolves disputes but fosters respect, trust, and collaboration among team members.

- **Understanding Compassionate Conflict Management**

Compassionate conflict management is an approach where empathy and understanding are at the forefront.

Rather than focusing solely on the resolution, this method prioritizes addressing the underlying emotions and motivations of all parties involved.

By doing so, it creates an environment where individuals feel heard, valued, and respected.

- **Steps to Practice Compassionate Conflict Management**

1. Listen Actively
   - Take the time to listen to all parties without interruption. Active listening involves maintaining eye contact, nodding to

acknowledge understanding, and paraphrasing key points to ensure clarity.

- **Example:** If two colleagues have opposing views on a project strategy, give each person a chance to explain their stance fully before responding.

2. Acknowledge Emotions

- Emotions often fuel conflicts. Acknowledging these emotions can defuse tension and create a sense of safety.

- **Example:** Saying, "I can see that you're frustrated, and that's valid," shows empathy and encourages open dialogue.

3. Focus on Interests, Not Positions

- Often, conflicts are rooted in differing interests rather than the positions people take.

Identifying these interests can reveal common ground.

   - **Example:** In a scheduling dispute, instead of arguing over specific days, focus on why each person prefers those days. This might uncover flexible solutions.

4. Communicate Clearly
   - Focus on facts, avoiding inflammatory or confrontational tone. Frame feedback and concerns constructively.

   - **Example:** Instead of saying 'You're always late,' try reframing it as 'I've noticed some delays. What corrective actions can we take to get the project back on schedule and achieve our goals?"

5. Seek Collaborative Solutions

- Involve all parties in brainstorming solutions that satisfy everyone's needs. By working together, individuals develop a sense of accountability and investment in the outcome.

- **Example:** If a team disagrees on resource allocation, collectively prioritize tasks to ensure fairness and efficiency.

6. Follow Up

- Post-conflict, schedule a follow-up to assess the outcome, provide additional support if needed, and confirm that all parties are satisfied.

- **Example:** Schedule a check-in meeting a week after a resolution to assess progress and address any new concerns.

- **The Benefits of Compassionate Conflict Management**

1. Improved Relationships

- By addressing conflicts with empathy and understanding, you strengthen trust and camaraderie among colleagues.

- **Example:** A manager who mediates disputes fairly gains the respect and loyalty of their team.

2. Increased Productivity

- Resolving conflicts quickly and compassionately reduces distractions and allows teams to focus on their goals.

- **Example:** A quick resolution to a disagreement over task roles ensures a project stays on track.

3. Enhanced Emotional Intelligence

- Practicing compassionate conflict management develops key emotional intelligence skills, such as empathy, self-regulation, and social awareness.

- **Example:** Handling a heated conversation calmly showcases emotional maturity and professionalism.

4. A Positive Workplace Culture

- When compassion becomes a norm, it creates a culture where employees feel safe and supported, fostering collaboration and innovation.

- **Example:** A company known for empathetic leadership often attracts and retains top talent.

- **Empowering Habits to Build Compassionate Conflict Management**

1. Develop Self-Awareness

- Reflect on your triggers and biases to approach conflicts neutrally.

- Practice mindfulness techniques, such as deep breathing, to stay composed during challenging conversations.

2. Enhance Communication Skills

- Engage in workshops or courses focused on effective communication. Skills like paraphrasing, summarizing, and asking open-ended questions are invaluable.

3. Cultivate Empathy

- Make a habit of viewing situations from others' perspectives. Regularly practicing empathy in small interactions prepares you for larger conflicts.

4. Encourage Feedback

- Create a safe and supportive space where team members can give and receive feedback without hesitation, promoting growth and improvement. This approach mitigates misunderstandings and prevents conflicts from spiraling out of control.

Compassionate conflict management is more than just resolving disagreements; it's about building bridges, fostering understanding, and creating a harmonious workplace.

CHAPTER 6

DEVELOPING SELF AWARENESS AND SOCIAL SKILLS FOR PERSONAL GROWTH

Success in the workplace is closely tied to understanding oneself and building strong relationships with others.

Self-awareness and social skills are essential tools that empower individuals to navigate professional environments effectively, foster collaboration, and achieve personal and organizational goals.

- **Understanding Self-Awareness**

Self-awareness involves recognizing and interpreting your internal experiences, including emotions, thoughts, and motivations.

It serves as the foundation for personal growth because it allows you to identify your strengths, weaknesses, and triggers.

Developing self-awareness involves consistent reflection and a willingness to embrace feedback.

- **Practical Steps to Enhance Self-Awareness:**

1. Maintain a Journal: Writing down your daily experiences, emotions, and thoughts can help identify patterns in your behavior and reactions.

   - **Example:** Reflecting on why you felt frustrated during a team meeting might reveal a need for better communication or clearer expectations.

2. Seek Feedback: Asking colleagues, supervisors, or mentors for constructive feedback can provide valuable insights into how others perceive you.

-**Example:** A coworker may point out your strong problem-solving skills while suggesting improvements in time management.

- **Building Social Skills**

Social skills are the abilities that enable effective communication, empathy, and collaboration.

In the workplace, these skills are critical for establishing trust and maintaining positive relationships.

- **Key Social Skills for Workplace Success:**

1. Active Listening: Paying attention, asking questions, and showing genuine interest in others' perspectives demonstrates respect and builds rapport.

   - **Example:** During a team discussion, paraphrase a colleague's point to confirm understanding, such as, "So, you're suggesting we approach the project with a phased timeline, right?"

2. Empathy: Understanding and sharing the feelings of others fosters a supportive and cooperative environment.

   - **Example:** When a teammate struggles with a tight deadline, showing understanding and offering help can boost morale and strengthen team dynamics.

3. Conflict Resolution: Addressing disagreements constructively requires patience, clear communication, and a focus on solutions rather than blame.

-**Example:** If two team members have differing ideas about a project, facilitate a meeting where each can express their views and work together to find a compromise.

4. Adaptability: The ability to adjust your communication style to suit different individuals or situations makes you a versatile and effective team member.

- **Example:** A technical explanation may require simplification when presenting to a non-technical audience.

- **Combining Self-Awareness and Social Skills for Personal Growth**

Building self-awareness and social skills is an iterative and continuous process that evolves over time with experience, learning, and self-reflection.

These skills complement each other and enhance your capacity to navigate challenges and seize opportunities.

For instance, self-awareness helps you recognize how your behavior impacts others, while social skills enable you to adjust accordingly.

Imagine receiving feedback from your manager about missing a project deadline.

A self-aware individual would first acknowledge the emotions triggered by the feedback—whether it's defensiveness or embarrassment—and then shift focus to the constructive aspects.

Using social skills, they might respond by thanking the manager for their input and discussing ways to improve time management in the future.

- **Empowering Habits for Workplace Success**

To integrate these skills into daily life, cultivate habits that reinforce both self-awareness and social skills:

- Set aside time each week for self-reflection and planning.

- Make an effort to connect with colleagues by showing interest in their work and lives.

- Practice humility by accepting mistakes and learning from them.

Personal growth is a journey, and mastering self-awareness and social skills is a significant step toward becoming a valuable contributor in any workplace.

These empowering habits not only enhance professional success but also foster a more fulfilling and balanced life.

RECOGNIZING AND MANAGING EMOTIONAL RESPONSES

In the workplace, emotions are often at the core of interactions and decision-making.

Recognizing and managing your emotional responses is crucial to fostering positive relationships, maintaining productivity, and navigating challenges effectively.

Emotional intelligence, the ability to understand and regulate one's emotions while empathizing with others, is a key habit for workplace success.

- **Recognizing Emotional Triggers**

The first step in managing emotions is to recognize what triggers them.

Triggers can include feedback from colleagues, tight deadlines, or a lack of acknowledgment for your efforts. To identify your emotional triggers:

- **Self-reflection:** Take time to review situations where you felt strong emotional reactions.

Journaling allows you to track and analyze your thoughts, emotions, and behaviors, uncovering recurring motifs and insights.

- **Ask for feedback:** Colleagues or mentors may observe patterns in your behavior that you haven't noticed.

- **Mindfulness:** Practice being present in the moment to recognize when your emotions are intensifying.

For instance, if a team meeting leaves you feeling undervalued, reflect on whether it's due to the tone of feedback, lack of participation, or personal insecurities. Having insight into your strengths, weaknesses, and habits enables you to make informed decisions about personal development.

- **Managing Emotional Responses**

Once you've identified your emotional triggers, the next step is developing strategies to manage your reactions constructively.

1. Pause Before Reacting

A brief pause can prevent impulsive reactions that may escalate conflicts. For example, if you receive a critical email, take a few minutes to process the message before replying.

This gives you time to compose a thoughtful response instead of reacting defensively.

2. Reframe Your Perspective

Try to view situations from a neutral or positive angle. Instead of seeing critical feedback as a personal attack, interpret it as an opportunity for growth.

This shift can reduce negative emotions and promote a problem-solving mindset.

3. Develop Healthy Outlets

Physical activity, creative hobbies, or talking to a trusted confidant can help diffuse pent-up emotions.

For example, a quick walk during lunch can alleviate stress from a demanding morning.

4. Communicate Effectively

Share your emotions in a clear and professional manner. Communicate your feelings effectively by using 'I' statements, which help to avoid accusations and defensiveness.

For instance, Focusing on personal feelings and experiences, instead of attacking others, helps to address issues in a clear and respectful manner.

- **Building Resilience to Emotional Stress**

In addition to managing immediate emotional responses, building long-term resilience is essential for workplace success.

- **Cultivate gratitude:** Focusing on the positive aspects of your work life, such as supportive colleagues or successful projects, can buffer against stress.

- **Strengthen relationships:** Strong workplace connections foster trust and emotional support during challenging times.

- **Prioritize self-care:** Adequate sleep, a balanced diet, and regular exercise enhance emotional regulation and overall well-being.

- **Applying Emotional Awareness to Workplace Scenarios**

Imagine a scenario where a team member critiques your presentation during a meeting.

Recognizing your initial emotional response—perhaps frustration or embarrassment—allows you to pause and avoid an immediate defensive reaction.

Instead, you could say, "I value your opinion; I'll take your comments into account and adjust accordingly."

This not only maintains professionalism but also demonstrates openness to collaboration.

Another example is handling stress during a major project. Recognize that tight deadlines are triggering anxiety, and use techniques like breaking tasks into smaller steps, delegating responsibilities, and practicing deep breathing exercises.

Managing emotions effectively ensures you remain focused and composed under pressure.

Recognizing and managing emotional responses is an empowering habit that fosters workplace success.

USING EMPATHY TO STRENGTHEN CONNECTIONS

Empathy is a powerful skill that transforms workplace dynamics, fostering deeper connections among colleagues, enhancing communication, and creating a more collaborative environment.

It's not just about understanding others' emotions but also about actively engaging with their perspectives to build trust and mutual respect.

- **The Role of Empathy in Workplace Success**

Empathy enables professionals to connect on a human level. When team members feel valued and understood, they are more likely to engage actively, share ideas openly, and contribute to a positive workplace culture.

This creates an environment where creativity thrives, conflicts are resolved efficiently, and productivity improves.

For example, imagine a situation where a team member constantly misses deadlines. Instead of assuming laziness or disorganization, an empathetic approach would involve a private conversation to understand their challenges.

Perhaps they're struggling with a workload imbalance or personal issues.

Addressing the root cause not only solves the immediate problem but also builds trust, showing the employee that their well-being matters.

- **Building Empathy in the Workplace**

1. Show Genuine Interest

Take time to understand your colleagues' goals, challenges, and personal interests.

Simple acts like remembering their favorite coffee order or acknowledging their contributions in meetings can build rapport and trust.

2. Adapt Your Communication Style

Tailor your interactions to suit the preferences and needs of others. If someone prefers written communication over verbal, respect that choice. Empathy involves meeting people where they are, not where you want them to be.

- **Empathy in Action: Case Study**

During a project crunch, a manager noticed a team member seemed unusually quiet in meetings.

Instead of pressing them to contribute, the manager approached them privately and learned that the individual was struggling with burnout.

By redistributing some of their tasks and encouraging time off, the manager not only helped the employee recover but also earned their loyalty and boosted overall team morale.

This kind of empathetic leadership ensures that team members feel supported, which translates to higher retention rates and a more harmonious workplace.

- **Long-Term Benefits of Empathy**

1. Stronger Team Collaboration

Empathy reduces misunderstandings and fosters a collaborative spirit. Teams with empathetic members work seamlessly, leveraging diverse perspectives.

2. Enhanced Leadership

Empathetic leaders inspire trust, improve morale, and build teams that are resilient under pressure.

3. Conflict Resolution

By understanding each party's perspective, conflicts can be resolved amicably and productively.

4. Increased Employee Engagement

When employees feel understood, they are more motivated to contribute to the organization's success.

Using empathy to strengthen connections is not just a personal virtue but a professional advantage.

It cultivates a workplace where people feel seen, heard, and valued, paving the way for collective success.

MANAGING STRESS IN HIGH-PRESSURE SITUATIONS

High-pressure situations at work can be daunting, especially when deadlines loom or unexpected challenges arise.

However, managing stress effectively in these scenarios is crucial for maintaining productivity, emotional well-being, and overall workplace success.

Adopting empowering habits can help you navigate stress with resilience and clarity.

1. Prioritize Tasks Strategically

One of the most effective ways to handle stress in high-pressure situations is to organize and prioritize tasks.

Use a simple yet powerful framework like the **urgent-important matrix** to categorize tasks based on urgency and importance. Focus on high-priority items first and delegate or delay less critical tasks.

Suppose you're a project manager coordinating the various aspects of introducing a new product to the market. Breaking down the project into smaller milestones and tackling critical tasks first can prevent overwhelm.

For example, address major technical issues before diving into secondary marketing materials.

2. Master Time Management

Time management is a key skill in managing workplace stress. Avoid overloading your schedule and use practical tools like digital calendars or task lists. Allocate specific blocks of time to important projects and stick to them.

If you're leading a team meeting, set a 30-minute limit and focus only on key discussion points. This helps streamline the meeting and allows time for other pressing matters.

3. Develop a Resilience Mindset

Resilience is about adapting to challenges without losing focus. Cultivating a growth mindset—believing that challenges are opportunities for learning—can transform how you perceive pressure.

Practice mindfulness techniques, such as controlled breathing or brief meditation, to stay present and calm during tense moments.

When a critical system crashes during an important presentation, taking a few deep breaths before addressing the problem helps you maintain composure and find a quick solution.

4. Leverage Team Collaboration

High-pressure situations often demand teamwork. Rely on your colleagues by fostering open communication and sharing responsibilities. Delegating tasks not only reduces personal stress but also empowers your team.

During a sudden surge in customer queries, divide responsibilities among team members based on their expertise.

For instance, have tech-savvy colleagues handle technical questions while others focus on general inquiries.

5. Maintain a Healthy Work-Life Balance

Sustaining a work-life balance is essential for managing stress long-term.

Make time for activities outside of work that rejuvenate your energy—whether it's exercising, pursuing hobbies, or spending quality time with loved ones.

An employee who works long hours might find relief in setting aside 30 minutes daily for a brisk walk or yoga. These activities can clear the mind and improve focus at work.

6. Reframe Stress as a Motivator

Not all stress is bad. Sometimes, it can act as a catalyst for peak performance when approached correctly.

Reframing stress as a sign of importance and urgency rather than danger can help you channel it productively.

A sales representative preparing for a major pitch can view the pressure as an opportunity to showcase their expertise, using it to fuel preparation and sharpen focus.

CHAPTER

7

MANAGING STRESS AND AVOIDING BURNOUT

In the late 19th century, as industrialization reshaped the modern workforce, factory workers toiled for long hours in unforgiving conditions.

This era saw the birth of the term "burnout," not as we know it today, but in the physical sense—machines overheated and broke down under excessive strain.

By the mid-20th century, researchers began to draw parallels between those mechanical breakdowns and the human experience in demanding work environments.

The term "burnout" was officially coined in the 1970s, describing a state of chronic stress and emotional exhaustion.

Today, workplace stress and burnout are recognized as serious issues that hinder productivity, creativity, and overall well-being.

- **Understanding Stress in the Modern Workplace**

Stress in the workplace often arises from a combination of factors—tight deadlines, high expectations, interpersonal conflicts, and the constant demand to perform.

While a manageable level of stress can motivate and energize, excessive stress can lead to burnout, which manifests as mental fatigue, disengagement, and declining job performance.

- **Strategies for Managing Stress**

1. Time Management Techniques

Effective time management reduces stress by helping you prioritize tasks and avoid feeling overwhelmed. Tools like to-do lists, calendar planning, and task delegation are invaluable.

For instance, breaking a large project into smaller, actionable steps not only makes it more manageable but also provides a sense of achievement as you complete each phase.

2. Creating Healthy Boundaries

Establishing boundaries is essential to maintaining a healthy work-life balance.

This includes learning to say no to unreasonable demands and setting clear expectations with colleagues and supervisors.

For example, turning off work-related notifications after office hours helps you recharge and avoid mental fatigue.

3. Physical and Mental Wellness

Incorporating regular exercise, maintaining a balanced diet, and practicing mindfulness techniques like meditation can significantly reduce stress.

Consider a manager who, despite a hectic schedule, dedicates 15 minutes daily to deep breathing exercises.

This simple habit can restore focus and calmness, even during the busiest days.

4. Seeking Support

Connecting with colleagues or a mentor provides an opportunity to share experiences and gain perspective.

Many organizations now offer employee assistance programs that provide access to counseling services.

For instance, during a challenging period, an employee might find relief by discussing workload issues with a supervisor who can help redistribute tasks.

- **Avoiding Burnout**

1. Recognizing Early Signs

Burnout doesn't happen overnight. It starts with subtle signs like irritability, lack of enthusiasm, and physical exhaustion.

Acknowledge these signs early and take corrective action. For instance, an employee who notices persistent tiredness might adjust their workload or take a short vacation to reset.

2. Maintaining Passion for Your Work

Invest your time and energy in endeavors that align with your core interests and abilities. Finding meaning in your work enhances motivation and reduces the risk of burnout.

For example, a graphic designer who feels overwhelmed with routine tasks might propose creative projects that reignite their passion for the job.

3. Building Resilience

Resilience involves coping with and rebounding from setbacks, trauma or significant stress. This involves developing coping strategies like focusing on solutions rather than problems, maintaining a positive outlook, and celebrating small victories.

A team leader, for example, might regularly acknowledge team accomplishments, fostering a culture of resilience and positivity.

4. Balancing Professional and Personal Goals

Pursuing hobbies, spending time with loved ones, and disconnecting from work are crucial for maintaining mental health.

A software developer who spends weekends hiking with family finds a renewed sense of purpose and energy upon returning to work.

Managing stress and avoiding burnout requires a proactive approach that prioritizes balance, self-care, and emotional awareness.

RECOGNIZING SIGNS OF STRESS EARLY

True success in the workplace begins not with the tasks you conquer, but with the stress you recognize and address.

By learning to see the quiet signs of strain within yourself and others, you unlock the power to create balance, nurture resilience, and transform challenges into growth.

The strength to thrive lies in awareness—because what you ignore today may limit your potential tomorrow.

In today's fast-paced workplace, recognizing signs of stress early can significantly impact productivity and personal well-being.

Stress is often seen as a silent disruptor, gradually affecting physical health, emotional stability, and work performance.

Being proactive in identifying these signs can help maintain a balanced, healthy approach to career success.

- **Physical Symptoms**

Stress often manifests physically before it becomes a noticeable mental or emotional burden. Common physical signs include fatigue, headaches, muscle tension, and digestive issues.

For instance, an employee constantly feeling drained despite getting adequate sleep may be experiencing stress-induced exhaustion.

Similarly, frequent headaches or stomach discomfort can indicate underlying workplace anxiety.

- **Emotional and Behavioral Indicators**

Emotionally, stress can cause irritability, mood swings, or feelings of overwhelm.

You might notice a normally optimistic colleague becoming unusually pessimistic or withdrawn.

Behavioral changes, such as increased absenteeism, procrastination, or difficulty concentrating, are also red flags.

Imagine a team member who once thrived under tight deadlines suddenly struggling to meet even basic expectations—this could be a sign of mounting stress.

- **Professional Performance**

Stress can erode professional performance over time. Missed deadlines, lower-quality work, or a decline in creativity are key indicators.

For instance, an otherwise high-performing individual might start turning in incomplete reports or exhibit a lack of attention to detail.

Recognizing these patterns early can help prevent further decline and mitigate workplace challenges.

- **Strategies to Recognize Stress Early**

1. Self-Awareness Practices: Regularly checking in with yourself can help you identify stress triggers.

Journaling about your daily experiences or practicing mindfulness can reveal stress patterns.

2. Observation: Supervisors and peers should remain attentive to changes in team dynamics.

If someone starts isolating themselves or their attitude shifts drastically, it may be worth addressing the issue privately.

3. Open Communication: Encourage honest conversations about workloads, expectations, and challenges.

For instance, a team meeting that allows employees to express concerns constructively can often uncover hidden stressors.

- **Real-Life Example**

Take the case of a marketing executive tasked with overseeing multiple campaigns simultaneously.

Despite her enthusiasm, the increasing workload led to sleepless nights and a short temper at work.

By acknowledging her irritability and physical fatigue, she realized the need to delegate tasks and discuss her workload with her manager. Early intervention prevented further burnout and helped her regain balance.

- **Importance of Early Recognition**

Recognizing stress early is not just about preventing burnout; it's about fostering a supportive workplace culture.

PRACTICING MINDFULNESS AND RELAXATION

Success in the workplace is not just about achieving goals—it's about mastering the art of being present.

When you quiet the chaos within, focus sharpens, creativity flows, and resilience becomes your greatest strength.

Mindfulness and relaxation aren't distractions; they are the foundation of sustained excellence.

In today's fast-paced work environment, stress and pressure often become part of the daily routine.

However, practicing mindfulness and relaxation can transform how you navigate workplace challenges, boosting productivity, creativity, and overall satisfaction.

Incorporating these practices into your professional life can help you stay focused, resilient, and balanced.

- **What Is Mindfulness and Why It Matters**

Mindfulness involves staying present and fully engaged in the moment, without judgment.

It's about paying attention to your thoughts, feelings, and environment without letting them overwhelm you.

In the workplace, this can mean being aware of how you approach tasks, interact with colleagues, and respond to stressors.

For instance, during a stressful meeting, practicing mindfulness might involve focusing on your breath, actively listening to others, and pausing before responding.

This creates a calm and thoughtful atmosphere, making communication more effective.

- **Simple Techniques for Workplace Mindfulness**
  - ❖ **Mindful Breathing**

  Take a few minutes to focus on your breathing. Sit comfortably at your desk, close your eyes, and breathe deeply in through your nose and out through your mouth.

  Count to four as you inhale and exhale. This simple act can center your mind and reduce stress.

  Example: Before giving a presentation, spend two minutes practicing deep breathing. It can calm your nerves and improve your delivery.

  - ❖ **Body Scanning**

  At regular intervals during the day, perform a mental body scan. Starting at your head and working down to your feet, notice areas of tension and consciously relax them.

This helps relieve physical stress often caused by long hours of sitting or standing.

Example: After a demanding phone call, take a moment to relax your shoulders and neck, releasing built-up tension.

❖ **Single-Tasking**

Multitasking might feel productive, but it often leads to errors and burnout. Instead, focus on one task at a time with full attention. Completing tasks mindfully improves efficiency and quality.

Example: When replying to emails, avoid switching between tabs. Dedicate specific time blocks to email responses.

- **Relaxation Practices for a Balanced Workday**

Relaxation complements mindfulness by helping you unwind and recharge. Here are some practical ways to incorporate relaxation into your workday:

- **Short Breaks for Resetting**

Take short, intentional breaks to disconnect from work. Step outside for fresh air, stretch, or enjoy a cup of tea. These small moments can refresh your mind.

Example: Set a timer to remind yourself to stand and stretch every hour. It boosts circulation and prevents fatigue.

- **Desk-Friendly Relaxation Exercises**

Incorporate simple exercises like shoulder rolls, seated stretches, or progressive muscle relaxation. These activities don't require leaving your desk and can ease physical tension.

Example: After typing for an hour, stretch your wrists and fingers to prevent strain.

- **Visualization Techniques**

Visualization involves imagining a peaceful scene or positive outcome. Close your eyes and picture a serene beach, a forest, or your ideal workday. This helps reduce stress and inspires motivation.

Example: Before tackling a challenging project, visualize successfully completing it with confidence.

Creating a Mindful Workplace Culture
Encouraging mindfulness and relaxation practices within your team can foster a

healthier and more productive work environment.

Share these techniques with colleagues, schedule group meditation sessions, or set up a quiet space for reflection.

Over time, these habits can reshape the workplace dynamic, making it more supportive and empowering.

Practicing mindfulness and relaxation at work is not about adding more tasks to your to-do list—it's about enhancing how you approach your existing responsibilities.

ACHIEVING WORK-LIFE BALANCE

Imagine standing in the middle of a crowded park, juggling brightly colored balls.

Each ball represents a piece of your life—your career, family, health, hobbies, and friendships.

At first, the rhythm feels smooth, and the crowd cheers you on. But suddenly, someone tosses another ball your way—a new work project, an unexpected responsibility—and the pattern falters.

One by one, the balls threaten to tumble to the ground.
Now, picture a skilled juggler who doesn't just survive the chaos but thrives in it.

They know when to slow down, when to let a ball rest for a moment, and when to catch a new one with ease.

They focus on the rhythm, not the noise of the crowd. This balance doesn't come from magic—it comes from practice, strategy, and a willingness to adjust.

The same principle applies to work-life balance. Without intention and smart habits, we're all at risk of dropping the things that matter most.

But with a little planning, boundaries, and self-awareness, we can juggle the demands of life with poise and confidence, just like the master juggler. Ready to refine your skills and take control of your balance? Let's dive in!

Work-life balance is essential for maintaining productivity, personal well-being, and overall satisfaction in both professional and personal realms.

Achieving this balance requires intentional habits that empower individuals to excel at work while nurturing their personal lives.

Below are strategies to achieve this balance, supported by practical examples.

1. Set Clear Boundaries

One of the first steps to work-life balance is establishing boundaries between work and personal life. This means clearly defining when the workday begins and ends.

For instance, instead of checking emails late at night, dedicate specific hours to work tasks and stick to them.

Example:

Sophia, a project manager, noticed that constant notifications disrupted her family time. She began using "focus mode" on her phone during personal hours, ensuring work emails and calls didn't interrupt her evenings.

This simple habit allowed her to be present with her family while being more focused during work hours.

2. Prioritize Tasks with Smart Planning

A well-planned schedule reduces stress and creates room for personal activities.

Use techniques like time-blocking to ensure tasks are completed efficiently without unnecessary overtime.

Example:

David, a graphic designer, struggled with managing tight deadlines. He started each day by listing his top three priorities and allocating specific blocks of time to each.

This habit not only improved his efficiency but also gave him the freedom to leave work on time for his yoga class.

3. Learn to Delegate

Delegating tasks to capable team members reduces overburden and frees up time for strategic thinking and personal pursuits. Letting go of the "I need to do it all" mentality is crucial for balance.

Example:

Meena, a small business owner, used to manage every aspect of her business.

Realizing it was unsustainable, she hired a virtual assistant for administrative tasks. This gave her more time to focus on her family while growing her business.

4. Embrace Flexible Work Practices

Flexibility is a key enabler of balance. Whether it's remote work or adjusting work hours, flexibility allows individuals to align work with personal priorities.

Example:

John, an IT specialist, negotiated a hybrid work schedule with his employer, allowing him to work from home two days a week.

He used this time to help his kids with their schoolwork while maintaining his job responsibilities.

5. Develop Stress-Relief Routines

Stress management is integral to work-life balance.

Building habits like regular exercise, meditation, or creative hobbies can help alleviate work-related pressure.

Example:

Emma, a marketing professional, started a daily habit of taking a 15-minute walk after lunch.

This brief activity cleared her mind and made her afternoons more productive, helping her leave work on time without feeling overwhelmed.

6. Communicate Openly

Open communication with managers, colleagues, and family about your needs and limitations fosters mutual understanding and support.

Example:

Michael, a software engineer, informed his manager about his need to leave by 5 PM for evening classes.

By communicating early, he managed his workload effectively and achieved his personal development goals.

CHAPTER 8

HARNESSING CREATIVITY AND INNOVATION

How can cultivating simple daily habits turn you into a powerhouse of creativity and innovation at work?

By adopting empowering habits like fostering a growth mindset, practicing curiosity, embracing diverse perspectives, and scheduling time for unstructured thinking, you can unlock untapped potential and drive groundbreaking solutions in your workplace.

For instance, something as simple as setting aside "innovation hours" or reflecting on past projects can transform routine tasks into opportunities for creative breakthroughs.

These practices not only enhance your personal effectiveness but also contribute to a vibrant, forward-thinking work culture that thrives on continuous improvement and adaptability.

In today's dynamic work environment, creativity and innovation are indispensable for success. They drive progress, encourage adaptability, and foster a culture of continuous improvement.

To empower yourself and others in the workplace, it is crucial to cultivate habits that nurture these qualities.

Below, we explore ways to integrate creativity and innovation into your daily professional routine.

1. Cultivate a Growth Mindset

A growth mindset encourages you to see challenges as opportunities to learn rather than obstacles.

This perspective fosters creative thinking by allowing you to take risks without the fear of failure.

Example:

Instead of viewing a tight deadline as a restriction, see it as an opportunity to brainstorm unconventional solutions.

An employee in a marketing firm once turned a last-minute campaign request into a social media challenge, engaging audiences in real-time and exceeding the campaign's original goals.

2. Practice Curiosity Daily

Curiosity fuels innovation by pushing you to question norms and seek out new knowledge. Make it a habit to ask "why" or "what if" during routine tasks.

Example:

A team in product development reimagined their onboarding process by asking, "What if we could make this system more intuitive for new hires?" This led to the creation of an interactive app that halved onboarding time.

3. Embrace Diverse Perspectives

Working with individuals from different backgrounds introduces fresh viewpoints and sparks innovative ideas. Seek collaboration beyond your usual circle.

Example:

An HR manager involved employees from customer service in creating a new employee satisfaction survey.

Their frontline experience offered insights that transformed the questions, leading to actionable feedback.

4. Schedule "Unstructured" Time

Allot specific periods for free thinking without immediate goals. Creativity often emerges when you step away from rigid schedules.

Example:

A tech startup implemented weekly "innovation hours," allowing employees to work on any project they were passionate about.

This practice resulted in new product features that became major selling points.

5. Leverage Simple Tools for Brainstorming

Adopt accessible techniques like mind mapping or reverse brainstorming to uncover unique solutions.

Example:

During a workshop, a team used a reverse brainstorming technique to list ways to worsen customer satisfaction.

Then, they flipped those ideas into actionable improvements, resulting in enhanced service protocols.

6. Make Room for Reflection

Reflection helps you assess what worked, what didn't, and where improvements can be made.

Dedicate time to review completed projects and consider alternative approaches.

Example:

After a challenging product launch, a project manager facilitated a team-wide "lessons learned" meeting.

Insights from the discussion shaped a more streamlined approach for future projects.

7. Reward and Recognize Creativity

Acknowledging innovative ideas, no matter how small, motivates employees to think creatively. Establish a culture where creativity is celebrated and not overlooked.

Example:

A logistics company introduced a "Bright Ideas" board where employees could pin suggestions for process improvements.

Recognized ideas were rewarded with small incentives, boosting morale and operational efficiency.

THINKING OUTSIDE THE BOX IN PROBLEM-SOLVING

Imagine facing a stubborn challenge at work—one that seems to resist every standard solution. Frustrating, right?

Now picture yourself flipping the problem on its head, discovering a fresh perspective, and creating a breakthrough solution that leaves everyone impressed. That's the magic of thinking outside the box.

In today's competitive workplace, it's not enough to rely on tried-and-true methods. Employers and teams value individuals who can tackle problems in unique, innovative ways.

Whether you're brainstorming new ideas, overcoming roadblocks, or inspiring a team, the ability to think differently is your ultimate edge.

This guide dives deep into how you can develop the habit of thinking outside the box and why it's a game-changer for workplace success. Packed with relatable examples and practical strategies, you'll learn how to:

- ❖ Break free from assumptions holding you back.

- ❖ Foster creativity through diverse perspectives and fearless brainstorming.

- ❖ Experiment confidently, even in the face of potential failure.

- ❖ Recharge your mind for fresh insights.

By the time you're done, you'll not only have a sharper approach to problem-solving but also the tools to stand out in your career.

Dive in to discover how empowering this habit can be—and start transforming challenges into opportunities today.

In today's fast-paced and ever-changing workplace, traditional approaches to problem-solving are often insufficient.

Thinking outside the box—approaching challenges in unconventional and innovative ways—is an empowering habit that can lead to significant workplace success.

This mindset pushes individuals to step away from the usual methods, question assumptions, and embrace creativity.

- **What Does Thinking Outside the Box Mean?**

Thinking outside the box involves looking at problems from fresh perspectives and exploring solutions that might initially seem unconventional.

It's about breaking free from habitual thought patterns and being open to experimenting with new ideas.

This habit encourages flexibility, critical thinking, and adaptability—traits that are highly valued in any professional environment.

- **Strategies to Develop This Habit**
  - ❖ **Challenge Assumptions**

Many workplace problems persist because of unchallenged assumptions.

For instance, if a team constantly misses deadlines, the assumption might be that they need to work harder.

By questioning this belief, you might uncover the real issue—inefficient processes or unclear expectations.

Example: When a retail company faced declining sales, instead of blaming external factors, a team leader questioned whether their marketing strategies resonated with current customer preferences.

This led to a complete overhaul of their approach, resulting in increased engagement and revenue.

- **Brainstorm Without Judgment**

Create a habit of brainstorming freely without immediately evaluating ideas. This technique allows team members to share even the wildest ideas without fear, fostering a creative atmosphere.

Often, solutions that initially seem impractical can be refined into actionable plans.

Example: A software development team brainstorming new features allowed all suggestions, from small tweaks to ambitious overhauls.

One unusual idea—letting users customize workflows—became their most popular feature.

- **Seek Diverse Perspectives**

Collaborating with individuals from different departments, backgrounds, or industries can spark ideas you may not have considered.

Example: A marketing manager working on a campaign invited the customer support team to provide input.

Their insights, based on direct customer interactions, helped tailor the campaign for better resonance with the audience.

- **Experiment and Embrace Failure**

Fear of failure often stifles creativity. Develop a habit of experimenting with small-scale tests to explore new solutions. Even if an idea doesn't work, it can provide valuable insights.

Example: A manufacturing company tested using recycled materials in its production process. While the first attempt failed due to quality issues, iterative testing eventually led to a cost-effective and eco-friendly solution.

- **Take Breaks to Recharge Creativity**

Overworking can drain creative energy. Encourage breaks and activities that stimulate the mind, such as reading, exercising, or exploring unrelated hobbies. These habits can help you approach problems with a refreshed perspective.

Example: A project manager stuck on a scheduling conflict found clarity after stepping away for a walk.

The solution, a slight adjustment in resource allocation, seemed obvious with a fresh mind.

- **Benefits of Thinking Outside the Box**
- ❖ **Enhanced Problem-Solving:** Innovative thinking leads to more effective and sustainable solutions.

- ❖ **Increased Confidence:** Successfully addressing challenges creatively builds confidence in your abilities.

- ❖ **Team Collaboration:** Encouraging a culture of innovation fosters teamwork and mutual respect.

- ❖ **Career Growth:** Professionals known for their ability to think creatively often stand out, making them strong candidates for leadership roles.

Developing the habit of thinking outside the box isn't just about solving problems; it's about fostering a mindset of continuous improvement and innovation.

EMBRACING CHANGE AND STAYING AGILE

In the ever-evolving workplace, one thing is certain—change is inevitable. Whether it's adopting new technologies, pivoting to meet industry demands, or navigating organizational shifts, success belongs to those who can adapt and excel under pressure. But how do you stay ahead without feeling overwhelmed?

This article unlocks the secrets to embracing change and staying agile, revealing practical habits that empower you to not only survive but thrive in today's dynamic professional landscape.

Imagine being the one who effortlessly navigates challenges, seizes opportunities, and stands out as a leader in your field.

From real-world examples to actionable steps, you'll discover how to:

- Shift from fearing change to leveraging it as an advantage.

- Build habits like curiosity, flexibility, and emotional intelligence that fuel your success.

- Approach workplace transformations—big or small—with confidence and resilience.

Packed with insights and relatable scenarios, this guide is your roadmap to staying relevant and indispensable in a world that refuses to stand still.

Ready to turn challenges into opportunities and make your superpower agility? Keep reading and take the first step toward your next breakthrough.

In today's fast-paced workplace, embracing change and staying agile are no longer optional—they are vital for success.

Businesses evolve, technology advances, and industry trends shift. Those who adapt quickly and effectively are often the ones who thrive.

Developing empowering habits that enhance your adaptability can significantly improve your professional resilience.

- **The Importance of Embracing Change**

Change can be intimidating. Whether it's a new company policy, a shift in leadership, or the adoption of new technology, it challenges us to step out of our comfort zones.

However, resisting change can lead to stagnation. Embracing change not only helps you stay relevant but also positions you as a proactive and forward-thinking professional.

For instance, when a team transitions to a new project management tool, those who invest time in learning its features and applying them effectively will likely perform better than those who cling to outdated systems.

This habit of approaching change with curiosity rather than fear can make you a valuable asset to your organization.

- **Building Habits for Agility**

Agility in the workplace is the ability to pivot and adjust strategies without losing momentum. To cultivate this skill, consider these empowering habits:

1. Stay Curious

Make a habit of continuous learning. This doesn't mean enrolling in endless courses but rather staying informed about industry trends, emerging tools, and best practices.

For example, if you're in marketing, understanding how algorithms affect digital advertising can keep you ahead of the curve.

2. Practice Flexibility

Instead of rigidly following a single approach, be open to exploring alternatives.

Flexibility allows you to navigate obstacles and seize opportunities that might otherwise go unnoticed.

For instance, if your current sales strategy isn't yielding results, experimenting with different techniques can lead to breakthroughs.

3. Cultivate a Growth Mindset

A growth mindset is the belief that abilities can be developed through effort and learning.

Viewing setbacks as opportunities to grow fosters resilience and adaptability. If a project fails, analyze what went wrong, learn from it, and apply those lessons to future initiatives.

4. Strengthen Emotional Intelligence

Adapting to change often involves working with diverse personalities and managing stress.

Emotional intelligence—understanding and managing your emotions while empathizing with others—helps you maintain strong workplace relationships even during turbulent times.

- **Real-World Applications of Agility**

Consider the example of a mid-sized company undergoing digital transformation.

Employees were required to transition from paper-based workflows to cloud-based solutions.

Initially, many resisted the change, citing steep learning curves and disruptions to their routines.

However, those who embraced the shift by actively learning the new system, asking questions, and experimenting with its features quickly outperformed their peers.

Their agility not only improved their productivity but also positioned them for leadership opportunities in the newly digitized workplace.

- **Steps to Empower Yourself Through Change**

1. Anticipate Change

Rather than waiting for change to catch you off guard, anticipate it. Stay updated on company goals, industry innovations, and economic trends.

2. Seek Support Networks

Collaborate with mentors, colleagues, or professional groups who can guide you through transitions. Collective problem-solving often sparks innovative solutions.

3. Celebrate Small Wins

Change can feel overwhelming, but breaking it into manageable steps and celebrating progress boosts confidence.

For instance, mastering a new skill or successfully completing a challenging project are milestones worth acknowledging.

In an ever-changing workplace, the ability to adapt is one of the most empowering habits you can develop.

LEVERAGING INNOVATION TO STAND OUT

You're standing in a bustling coffee shop on a Monday morning, the kind where everyone is hustling for their caffeine fix. Amid the chatter and chaos, you notice two employees behind the counter.

One follows the routine—mechanically taking orders and handing out drinks. The other, however, is doing something different.

They're cracking jokes, suggesting drink combinations customers hadn't considered, and even finding quicker ways to serve the long line. People gravitate toward them, leaving with a smile and a story to tell.

Now, think about your workplace. Are you the employee sticking to the script, or are you the one bringing innovation, creativity, and personality into your role?

The difference between blending in and standing out lies in small, deliberate habits that foster innovation and make you unforgettable.

What if you could take those moments of playful ingenuity and turn them into a consistent advantage in your career?

This guide will show you how to adopt the habits of the second barista—making every interaction, every task, and every challenge an opportunity to shine brighter than the crowd.

In today's competitive workplace, standing out is more about leveraging innovative thinking than relying on repetitive effort.

Cultivating empowering habits that foster creativity, adaptability, and problem-solving can set you apart in ways that make your contributions invaluable.

Here's how innovation plays a vital role in achieving workplace success and actionable steps to harness its potential.

1. Cultivate a Proactive Mindset
Instead of waiting for directions or following the status quo, proactive individuals anticipate challenges and devise creative solutions before issues arise.

For instance, imagine a team preparing for a product launch. A proactive individual might suggest integrating customer feedback from similar launches into the current strategy, ensuring fewer missteps and higher success rates.

Actionable Habit: Dedicate 15 minutes daily to brainstorming improvements in your area of responsibility. Focus on identifying gaps and proposing solutions to address them.

2. Embrace Lifelong Learning

Innovation thrives on fresh ideas, which often come from continuously learning and staying updated.

Whether it's learning a new software skill or diving into industry trends, expanding your knowledge ensures you're always contributing new perspectives.

Example: A marketing professional learns about the latest customer behavior analytics tools, helping their team create more targeted campaigns that outperform competitors.

Actionable Habit: Allocate time each week to read industry reports, take an online course, or attend a webinar. Reflect on how the insights gained can be applied in your role.

3. Adopt Design Thinking in Problem Solving

Design thinking—a systematic approach to problem-solving that prioritizes user experience—has revolutionized industries. You don't need to work in product development to use this method.

For instance, if a process in your department is slowing everyone down, applying design thinking can help uncover pain points and suggest innovative fixes.

Example: An HR manager redesigns the employee onboarding process by seeking input from recent hires, leading to a streamlined and more engaging experience for new recruits.

Actionable Habit: Approach problems by asking, "What is the user's perspective?" Then brainstorm ideas, prototype solutions, and test them for efficiency.

4. Foster Collaboration to Spark Innovation
Innovation doesn't happen in silos. Engaging with colleagues from different departments or disciplines can expose you to diverse viewpoints, often leading to breakthrough ideas.

Example: A finance team collaborates with IT to create an automated budgeting tool, reducing manual errors and saving hours of labor.

Actionable Habit: Schedule regular cross-departmental meetings or casual brainstorming sessions to encourage idea-sharing and collaboration.

5. Use Technology Strategically

Incorporating the right tools can streamline processes and boost productivity, but the key is to use them strategically.

For instance, leveraging workflow automation tools can free up time for more creative tasks.

Example: A project manager uses a project management platform to track tasks and deadlines, enabling the team to focus on strategic planning instead of administrative tasks.

Actionable Habit: Evaluate your daily tasks and identify repetitive processes that can be automated. Implement one new tool at a time to ensure a smooth transition.

6. Be Comfortable with Experimentation

Innovation requires taking calculated risks and learning from failures. In workplaces that prioritize growth, experimentation is often the gateway to discovering what works best.

Example: A sales team experiments with a new pitch format, testing its effectiveness with a small group of clients.

The insights gained are then used to refine the pitch before rolling it out company-wide.

Actionable Habit: Set up a small-scale experiment for a new idea every month. Document results and use the findings to make informed decisions.

7. Build an Agile Work Environment

Being adaptable and agile in your thinking ensures you're prepared to navigate unexpected changes.

For instance, when a company pivots its strategy, employees who can quickly align their efforts to new goals are often the ones who thrive.

Example: During a sudden shift to remote work, an employee adept at using virtual collaboration tools quickly becomes an essential team player.

Actionable Habit: Practice adaptability by routinely seeking feedback and adjusting your approach as needed. View change as an opportunity rather than a setback.

Leveraging innovation to stand out in the workplace isn't about grand gestures or revolutionary inventions.

It's about consistently adopting habits that promote creativity, collaboration, and a proactive approach to challenges.

By focusing on these empowering habits, you position yourself as a forward-thinking professional who not only contributes but also inspires others to embrace success.

CHAPTER

9

BUILDING A PROFESSIONAL IMAGE AND REPUTATION

In 1914, a young entrepreneur named Henry walked into a small factory, determined to transform not only his business but also his reputation.

His competitors doubted his potential, and his colleagues viewed him as inexperienced.

However, Henry understood something they didn't—your reputation is your currency in the professional world.

Through consistent habits such as punctuality, a keen eye for detail, and respect for colleagues, Henry built a professional image that ultimately secured him partnerships and a thriving enterprise.

His story reminds us that building a professional reputation is a journey fueled by deliberate actions.

Today, the stakes are higher, with workplace dynamics shaped by technology, competition, and the need for adaptability.

However, the foundation remains the same: empowering habits can transform not just your career trajectory but also how others perceive you.

1. Establishing the Foundations of a Professional Image

Your professional image is how others perceive you in the workplace—your attitude, behavior, and presentation all contribute.

Building this image starts with self-awareness and intentional habits that set you apart.

Dressing Appropriately: Your attire reflects your respect for the workplace culture.

For example, a creative professional may wear bold, stylish outfits, while someone in corporate settings might opt for formal, neutral tones. Understand your workplace norms and align your presentation with them.

Effective Communication: The way you speak and listen has a significant impact. Practice active listening during meetings and deliver clear, concise responses.

For instance, using plain language to explain a technical concept in a meeting can establish your competence.

Punctuality and Reliability: Consistently meeting deadlines and showing up on time builds trust.

If you've committed to completing a project by a specific date, ensure you deliver quality work promptly. A reputation for dependability earns long-term respect.

2. Building a Reputation Through Empowering Habits

Reputation grows from actions repeated over time. Your daily habits shape how colleagues, managers, and clients view your professional reliability and potential.

Exceeding Expectations: Always go the extra mile. For instance, instead of merely completing a report, include actionable recommendations that demonstrate foresight and initiative.

Demonstrating Integrity: Honesty and accountability are non-negotiable. Admit to mistakes when they occur and present solutions to rectify them. This habit not only shows professionalism but also garners trust.

Networking with Intent: Professional relationships are a cornerstone of a solid reputation.

Attend events, participate in team-building activities, and engage with colleagues.

For example, a quick coffee chat with a team member can lead to collaborations that highlight your strengths.

Skill Development: Continuously improve yourself by learning new skills relevant to your field.

Whether it's attending a workshop or mastering a new software tool, your willingness to grow reflects positively on your dedication.

3. Sustaining Your Professional Reputation Over Time

Building a reputation is one thing; maintaining it requires consistency, adaptability, and resilience.

Adaptability to Change: As workplace dynamics shift, your ability to adapt showcases your professionalism.

For example, when new technology is introduced, embrace it with a learning mindset rather than resistance.

Conflict Resolution: How you handle disagreements speaks volumes. Always approach conflicts with empathy and a focus on solutions.

For instance, if a team member misunderstands your email, clarify the issue calmly and in person to avoid escalation.

- ❖ Celebrating Small Wins: Acknowledge your achievements and those of your peers. Publicly appreciating a colleague's efforts fosters goodwill and reflects your supportive attitude.

- ❖ Seeking Feedback: Regularly request feedback from supervisors and colleagues to identify areas of improvement. This habit demonstrates humility and a commitment to growth.

Henry's story reminds us that professional success is not solely defined by talent but by the consistent habits we develop.

By dressing the part, communicating effectively, and embracing continuous learning, you build an image that commands respect.

Through integrity, collaboration, and adaptability, you nurture a reputation that opens doors to new opportunities.

In the modern workplace, your professional image and reputation serve as your personal brand.

By cultivating empowering habits, you set yourself on a path to enduring workplace success, leaving a legacy of excellence that will inspire others.

DEVELOPING TRUST AND CREDIBILITY

Trust is not granted but earned through consistency, transparency, and action; credibility is the unshakable foundation that turns intentions into influence.

Together, they form the bridge that transforms workplace interactions into lasting success.

In any professional setting, trust and credibility are essential for success. These qualities create an environment where collaboration thrives, decisions are respected, and individuals feel valued.

Building these traits doesn't happen overnight but is the result of consistent actions and empowering habits that demonstrate reliability, competence, and integrity.

- **Why Trust and Credibility Matter**

Trust is the foundation of every relationship in the workplace. It ensures that teams work cohesively, managers lead effectively, and clients remain loyal.

Credibility, on the other hand, underscores the belief in your expertise and dependability.

Together, they form a reputation that paves the way for leadership opportunities and long-term career growth.

- **Empowering Habits to Build Trust and Credibility**

Consistency in Actions Consistency demonstrates reliability. For example, if you commit to delivering a project by a deadline, ensure you meet it or communicate early if adjustments are needed.

Regularly keeping your word builds trust over time, showing that your promises are not hollow but actionable.

Transparency and Honesty Honesty fosters trust. In situations where a mistake is made, owning up to it and explaining the steps being taken to rectify it can enhance credibility.

For instance, admitting to a missed target in a team meeting and outlining a clear recovery plan showcases accountability and transparency.

Effective Communication Clear and empathetic communication builds trust by reducing misunderstandings and showing respect.

Listen actively to colleagues' concerns and respond thoughtfully. For example, instead of dismissing a team member's input in a meeting, acknowledge their perspective and build on it to show respect for their ideas.

Delivering Results Trust grows when you consistently deliver results. Meeting expectations—and sometimes exceeding them—reinforces your competence.

For instance, a graphic designer who consistently creates high-quality visuals ahead of deadlines will naturally become a go-to professional in their field.

Demonstrating Empathy Empathy creates connections and trust. When a colleague struggles with personal challenges, showing support or simply being a patient listener demonstrates care.

For instance, offering to cover a teammate's tasks during a family emergency not only builds trust but also fosters goodwill.

Developing Expertise Credibility stems from expertise. Continuously upskilling in your field ensures that others trust your judgment and decisions.

For example, a digital marketer who stays updated with the latest trends in social media algorithms will be seen as an expert and a credible source of advice.

Building Relationships Beyond Work Investing time in building personal rapport strengthens trust. Sharing interests or having informal conversations with colleagues humanizes professional relationships.

For instance, participating in team-building activities or showing interest in a coworker's hobby can bridge professional gaps.

Resolving Conflicts with Integrity Handling disputes with fairness and respect enhances credibility.

Avoiding bias and seeking win-win solutions ensures that others see you as a trustworthy mediator.

For example, addressing two team members' disagreements by facilitating an open discussion without taking sides builds confidence in your leadership.

- **Instances of Trust and Credibility in Action**
  - ❖ **Case 1:** The Dependable Team Member A software developer consistently delivered high-quality code and promptly addressed feedback.

When a critical client project arose, the manager entrusted the developer to lead, knowing their proven reliability.

  - ❖ **Case 2:** The Transparent Manager A department head informed the team about budget cuts affecting resources.

By openly sharing the challenges and collaborating on creative solutions, the manager not only maintained trust but also motivated the team to adapt effectively.

- **The Payoff**

Developing trust and credibility transforms workplace dynamics. Employees with these qualities often find themselves in leadership roles or entrusted with critical projects.

Teams led by such individuals perform better because of the supportive and dependable environment they create.

Trust and credibility are not just professional virtues but empowering habits that amplify workplace success.

NETWORKING WITH PURPOSE

True success in the workplace is not just about what you achieve, but the connections you cultivate with purpose.

Networking with authenticity transforms relationships into bridges of opportunity, where shared value and genuine engagement lead to growth, collaboration, and lasting impact.

Build with intention, nurture with care, and watch your professional world expand beyond limits.

Networking is more than exchanging business cards or connecting on professional platforms.

It's about cultivating meaningful relationships that can enhance your career, personal growth, and workplace success.

When approached with purpose, networking transforms from a transactional activity into a powerful tool for empowerment. Here's how to develop this habit effectively and authentically.

- **Understanding Purposeful Networking**

Purposeful networking means building relationships that align with your goals and values.

Unlike superficial connections, these relationships are grounded in mutual respect, shared interests, and long-term benefits.

For instance, if you aim to transition into project management, connecting with experienced project managers in your organization or industry can provide insights, mentorship, and opportunities.

The focus isn't solely on what you can gain but on creating a two-way relationship where you also offer value.

- **Key Habits for Purposeful Networking**

  ❖ **Set Clear Goals**

  Define your networking objectives. Are you looking to expand your industry knowledge, find mentors, or explore new opportunities? Having clear goals will guide your interactions and help you focus on meaningful relationships.

  Example: If you're new to a company, aim to meet colleagues in different departments to understand the organization's dynamics and broaden your perspective.

❖ Be Genuine

Authenticity is critical. People are more inclined to connect with those who show genuine interest in them.

Avoid approaching networking with a "what's in it for me" mindset. Instead, focus on learning about others' experiences, challenges, and successes.

Example: During a team lunch, instead of discussing tasks, ask a colleague about their career journey or a project they're passionate about.

❖ Follow Up and Stay Engaged

A connection isn't built in a single meeting. Regular follow-ups, whether through emails, casual check-ins, or social events, demonstrate that you value the relationship.

Example: After attending a seminar, follow up with a speaker or fellow attendee by sharing an article related to a topic discussed. This keeps the conversation alive and positions you as thoughtful and proactive.

- **Leverage In-House Networking**

Networking doesn't always mean reaching outside your workplace. Building relationships within your organization can lead to collaborations, mentorships, and career advancements.

Example: Participate in cross-departmental projects or volunteer for committees to connect with coworkers beyond your immediate team.

❖ **Attend Events with Intent**

Be selective about the networking events you attend. Choose events where you're likely to meet people aligned with your professional goals.

Prepare beforehand by researching attendees or speakers to identify potential connections.

Example: Instead of attending a general business mixer, join a panel discussion focused on emerging technologies in your field.

❖ The Power of Shared Value

Networking thrives on reciprocity. Think of it as an ecosystem where mutual support creates sustained growth.

Offer your expertise, share relevant resources, or provide introductions to people in your network.

This habit establishes you as a valuable connection, making others more willing to help when you need it.

Example: A former colleague reached out for advice on adapting to remote work.

Sharing your strategies and tools not only helped them but also strengthened your professional bond.

- **Overcoming Networking Challenges**

Some people find networking intimidating, especially in unfamiliar settings. Overcome this by focusing on smaller, actionable steps:

Start with one-on-one conversations.
Practice active listening to make others feel heard.

Use open-ended questions to encourage dialogue.

Example: At a conference, instead of nervously lingering, approach someone at a coffee table and ask, "What brought you to this event?"

- **The Role of Digital Networking**

In the modern workplace, digital networking is indispensable. Platforms like professional social media sites and industry-specific forums enable you to connect with peers globally.

- **Tips for Effective Digital Networking:**

Optimize your profile with clear, concise information about your expertise and goals.

Engage by commenting on posts, sharing insightful articles, or participating in discussions. Join online communities or webinars tailored to your field.

Example: Joining a virtual book club on leadership not only expands your network but also enhances your knowledge and adds to your credibility.

Networking with purpose is an empowering habit that can unlock countless opportunities for workplace success.

USING SOCIAL MEDIA FOR CAREER ADVANCEMENT

Your digital presence is more than a profile—it's a living testament to your ambitions, expertise, and potential.

When used with intention, social media transforms from a pastime into a powerful stage where your career unfolds, connections are forged, and success is no longer a distant dream but a daily habit. Master your online voice, and you'll master your professional journey.

In today's digital era, social media has transcended its original purpose of connecting friends and family to become a powerful tool for professional growth.

By leveraging the right platforms, individuals can showcase their skills, build meaningful networks, and stay updated with industry trends.

Here's how you can effectively use social media to advance your career while cultivating empowering habits for workplace success.

1. Curate a Professional Profile
Your online profile is often the first impression you make. Platforms like professional

networking sites and business-oriented social networks provide spaces to highlight your expertise. Keep your profile updated with:

- ❖ A professional headshot

- ❖ A concise yet impactful bio

- ❖ A detailed list of accomplishments and skills

- ❖ Regular updates showcasing your work, such as articles, projects, or achievements

For instance, if you're a graphic designer, sharing before-and-after visuals of your projects can attract attention from recruiters and peers alike.

2. Engage with Industry Leaders

Follow thought leaders, businesses, and organizations in your industry. Comment thoughtfully on their posts, share relevant content, and engage in discussions.

This habit not only builds your visibility but also positions you as someone genuinely interested in the field.

Example: A marketing professional can follow advertising agencies and engage in discussions about emerging trends like content personalization or AI in branding. Such contributions demonstrate knowledge and initiative.

3. Showcase Your Expertise Through Content

Becoming a content creator in your domain can set you apart. Write blogs, create how-to guides, record tutorials, or share insights about your industry.

Use platforms like content-sharing sites or video platforms to establish yourself as a credible voice.

Example: An IT professional can post simplified explanations of complex technologies, like how cloud computing benefits small businesses. This not only educates others but also displays your expertise.

4. Network Strategically

Social media allows you to connect with professionals across the globe. Approach networking with a strategic mindset:

- ❖ Personalize connection requests instead of sending generic messages.

- ❖ Reach out to professionals in roles or companies you aspire to join.

- ❖ Attend virtual events or join relevant groups for more interaction.

Example: If you're interested in working for a tech company, connecting with its employees and engaging with their posts can help you understand the culture and even get noticed during recruitment.

5. Stay Updated with Industry Trends
Follow hashtags and subscribe to accounts that regularly post about innovations and news in your field.

By staying informed, you can contribute more effectively to workplace discussions, demonstrate foresight, and position yourself as a forward-thinker.

Example: A finance professional following hashtags related to cryptocurrency trends can use that knowledge to propose new investment strategies at work.

6. Maintain Professionalism Online

Your digital footprint is a reflection of your personal brand. Adopt empowering habits like:

- ❖ Avoiding controversial topics unless they align with your professional stance

- ❖ Maintaining a respectful tone during debates

- ❖ Regularly auditing your past posts to ensure they reflect your current values and ambitions

Example: A teacher aiming for a leadership role in education might regularly share articles about innovative teaching methods while refraining from public criticism of educational policies.

7. Leverage Direct Messaging Wisely

Direct messaging is a powerful tool for networking when used appropriately. When reaching out to someone, keep your message brief, specific, and professional.

Example: Instead of a generic "Hi, I'd like to connect," try something like, "Hello, I admire your work in renewable energy, especially your recent article on solar panel efficiency.

I'm exploring opportunities in this field and would love to learn more about your journey."

8. Balance Personal and Professional Content

While it's important to showcase your personality, ensure that your personal posts do not overshadow your professional image.

Striking a balance can make you relatable without appearing unprofessional.

Example: Sharing a post about a community event you participated in can humanize your profile, while frequent posts about partying might not align with a professional image.

CHAPTER

10

BECOMING A LIFELONG LEARNER

History is rich with individuals who achieved greatness not because of innate talent but because of their relentless pursuit of learning.

Consider a celebrated American polymath, a self-taught individual who rose from humble beginnings to become a statesman, inventor, and author.

Despite having little formal education, this visionary cultivated a habit of lifelong learning.

He famously developed his personal system for self-improvement, dedicating time each day to study, reflection, and application.

His story demonstrates the transformative power of continuous learning and how it can propel anyone toward workplace success.

In today's world, lifelong learning is no longer a luxury—it's a necessity. The rapid pace of technological advancements and evolving industries demands a workforce that can adapt and grow.

Embracing lifelong learning is not merely about acquiring skills but fostering habits that empower success in any professional setting.

- **Key Habits to Cultivate Lifelong Learning for Workplace Success**

1. Set Clear Learning Goals
To become a lifelong learner, start with purpose. Define what you want to learn and why it matters to your career.

For instance, if you aspire to leadership roles, focus on developing skills like emotional intelligence, conflict resolution, and strategic thinking.

Clear goals give direction and motivation, making learning intentional rather than incidental.

Example: Sarah, a marketing professional, set a goal to master data analytics. She enrolled in online courses, attended webinars, and practiced with real-world datasets.

Her efforts not only enhanced her career prospects but also made her indispensable to her organization.

2. Develop a Growth Mindset

Psychologist Carol Dweck popularized the concept of a "growth mindset," the belief that abilities can be developed through effort and persistence.

Adopting this mindset encourages resilience in the face of challenges and mistakes.

Instead of seeing failure as a setback, view it as a stepping stone toward mastery.

Practical Tip: When learning something new, focus on progress rather than perfection.

Celebrate small wins and remind yourself that mastery is a journey, not a destination.

3. Leverage Microlearning

In a fast-paced workplace, finding time to learn can be challenging. Microlearning—breaking down information into manageable chunks—allows you to learn effectively without overwhelming your schedule.

Whether it's reading an article, watching a short tutorial, or listening to a podcast, these small learning sessions accumulate over time.

Example: John, a software developer, dedicated 20 minutes daily to learn a new programming framework. Within six months, he became proficient, leading to a promotion.

4. Seek Feedback and Act on It

Feedback is a powerful tool for growth. Constructive criticism from colleagues, mentors, or managers can highlight areas for improvement and guide your learning efforts.

Instead of taking feedback personally, use it as an opportunity to refine your skills.

Pro Tip: After completing a project, ask for specific feedback on what you did well and what could be improved.

This approach fosters continuous improvement and demonstrates your commitment to excellence.

5. Embrace Technology for Learning

Technology offers endless opportunities for personal and professional growth.

Online platforms, virtual courses, and skill-building apps provide accessible and affordable ways to upskill.

Make use of tools like Coursera, Skillshare, or Khan Academy to explore new areas of interest.

Example: Maria, an HR professional, used online platforms to learn about artificial intelligence and its application in recruitment.

Her newfound knowledge helped her implement innovative hiring strategies, earning her recognition in her field.

6. Practice What You Learn

Learning without application limits growth. The workplace provides a perfect environment to test and refine your skills.

Volunteer for challenging projects, take on new responsibilities, or mentor colleagues to solidify your learning.

Example: Alex, a project manager, attended a workshop on agile methodologies.

He applied these techniques in his next project, significantly improving team efficiency and project outcomes.

7. Stay Curious and Explore Beyond Your Field

Curiosity drives innovation. Don't limit your learning to your immediate job responsibilities.

Explore topics outside your field to gain fresh perspectives and insights that can be applied creatively to your work.

Example: A pioneering tech entrepreneur attributed much of his company's design innovation to a calligraphy class he attended.

His curiosity outside the digital world led to the beautiful typography used in his company's products.

8. Build a Supportive Network

Surround yourself with people who inspire and challenge you to grow.

A supportive network of mentors, peers, and industry professionals can provide guidance, encouragement, and accountability.

Pro Tip: Join professional associations or online communities where you can exchange ideas and learn from others in your field.

The workplace is a dynamic environment that rewards adaptability and growth.

THE IMPORTANCE OF CONTINUOUS EDUCATION

Imagine you're a gardener tending to a vibrant, ever-changing garden. Each plant represents a skill or piece of knowledge you've cultivated over time.

Some plants are thriving, others are wilting, and new seeds are waiting to be planted. But here's the twist—this garden doesn't stay the same.

The seasons shift unpredictably, and the soil constantly changes. The tools you used last year to grow tomatoes may now be obsolete for nurturing roses.

What's the secret to keeping this garden flourishing? It's not luck or a one-time effort—it's continuous care, learning, and adapting.

You read up on the latest gardening techniques, try out new fertilizers, and upgrade your tools.

Suddenly, what seemed like a chaotic, untamable plot transforms into a masterpiece of blooms, fruits, and greenery.

Your workplace success works in the same way. Without continuous education—your "watering can" and "gardening gloves"—your career garden risks stagnation.

But with consistent learning, you can grow not just a single flower bed of skills but an entire ecosystem of habits that adapt to any environment.

Dive into the article to uncover how lifelong learning empowers your workplace habits, turning your professional life into a flourishing, ever-relevant garden of growth and success!

In today's fast-paced and ever-changing work environment, continuous education is not just a personal choice; it's a professional necessity.

The ability to adapt, grow, and stay relevant is rooted in one's commitment to lifelong learning.

Continuous education enables employees to develop empowering habits that drive workplace success, fostering innovation, resilience, and adaptability.

- **Staying Ahead in a Competitive Landscape**

Industries are evolving rapidly due to advancements in technology and shifting market demands.

Employers value individuals who stay informed about these changes and can contribute meaningfully.

For instance, an IT professional who takes regular courses to stay updated on emerging technologies, such as cloud computing or cybersecurity, demonstrates their value as a forward-thinking employee.

This habit of self-improvement not only enhances career prospects but also inspires colleagues to adopt similar practices.

- **Cultivating a Growth Mindset**

Continuous education nurtures a growth mindset—a belief that skills and intelligence can be developed with effort and learning.

This mindset is essential for overcoming workplace challenges and seizing new opportunities.

For example, an entry-level marketing associate might feel intimidated by data analytics.

However, enrolling in a short course on analytics can build confidence and equip them with skills to create impactful campaigns.

This habit of proactively addressing weaknesses sets a strong foundation for long-term success.

- **Boosting Confidence and Competence**

When employees invest in learning, they gain deeper knowledge and better skills, which translate to greater confidence in their roles.

Take a customer service representative who pursues training in conflict resolution and emotional intelligence.

These new skills allow them to handle difficult situations effectively, improving both their performance and job satisfaction.

Regularly honing such capabilities empowers individuals to excel in their roles, ultimately contributing to organizational success.

- **Enhancing Adaptability and Innovation**

Continuous education enables individuals to remain agile in the face of change.

For instance, during the global shift to remote work, employees who sought training in digital tools and virtual collaboration were better equipped to navigate the new norm.

Their ability to adapt not only ensure personal success but also helped their organizations transition smoothly.

This adaptability fosters innovation, as employees feel encouraged to experiment with new ideas and solutions.

- **Practical Steps to Embed Continuous Education**

1. Leverage Online Platforms: Many accessible resources offer courses tailored to specific industries. Professionals can dedicate a few hours a week to expanding their knowledge.

2. Participate in Workshops and Seminars: Engaging with experts and peers provides fresh perspectives and practical insights.

3. Set Learning Goals: Identify areas for improvement or interest and create a structured plan to address them.

4. Seek Mentorship: Learning from experienced colleagues or industry leaders can accelerate growth and build professional networks.

- **Building Empowering Habits Through Learning**

Continuous education directly influences habits that lead to workplace success.

It fosters discipline, curiosity, and resilience—qualities essential for thriving in any professional setting.

Employees who prioritize learning demonstrate initiative and commitment, positioning themselves as indispensable assets to their teams.

Continuous education is the cornerstone of workplace success. It cultivates empowering habits that drive personal and professional growth, enabling individuals to remain competitive, confident, and adaptable.

SEEKING MENTORSHIP AND LEARNING OPPORTUNITIES

Imagine standing at the edge of a dense forest, a treasure map clutched tightly in your hand.

You know the treasure—a fulfilling, successful career—lies hidden deep within.

The map, however, is full of cryptic symbols and unmarked trails. Without guidance, the path seems daunting.

Now picture an experienced explorer stepping forward. They've been through this very forest, battled its challenges, and emerged victorious.

They show you how to read the map, warn you of the quicksand pits, and point out shortcuts you never would have noticed. That's your mentor—a guide who helps turn confusion into clarity.

As you journey forward, you find clues etched in the bark of ancient trees and in whispered tales from others you meet along the way.

These clues are your learning opportunities—insights and skills gained from trying new things, asking questions, and pushing past your comfort zone.

With every lesson learned, you mark another trail on your map, bringing the treasure closer.

The forest isn't as intimidating anymore. You're not alone, and every step forward feels more confident.

Together with your mentor's wisdom and the knowledge you've gathered, you carve your own path toward success, making the journey as rewarding as the destination.

This scene mirrors the power of mentorship and learning. Your mentor is the seasoned explorer, and the forest is your workplace—a realm full of challenges and opportunities.

With guidance and a thirst for growth, the treasure is well within reach. Will you take the first step?

One of the most empowering habits for workplace success is actively seeking mentorship and embracing learning opportunities.

In today's fast-evolving professional landscape, continuous growth and development are essential for staying competitive and achieving career goals.

By proactively connecting with experienced professionals and committing to lifelong learning, you can create a solid foundation for sustained success.

- **Why Mentorship Matters**

Mentorship provides a unique opportunity to gain insights and perspectives that go beyond textbooks and training courses.

A mentor is someone who has walked the path you're aspiring to follow. Their guidance can help you navigate challenges, avoid common pitfalls, and develop a clear sense of direction.

For example, imagine you're a junior software developer working to transition into a leadership role.

Finding a senior manager who has successfully made a similar leap can offer invaluable advice on managing teams, improving communication, and aligning your technical skills with strategic goals.

Regular mentorship meetings can also help you track your progress and adjust your approach as needed.

- **How to Find the Right Mentor**

To find a suitable mentor, start by identifying individuals who inspire you professionally.

These might be colleagues, industry leaders, or even professors from your educational journey.

Once identified, reach out to them with a clear and respectful request. For instance:

- **In-person connections:** Attend industry events, workshops, or networking sessions where you can meet potential mentors.

- **Digital outreach:** Use professional networking platforms like career-focused social networks or forums to connect with individuals whose expertise aligns with your goals.

When reaching out, be specific about why you admire their work and how their experience could guide your growth.

A message like, "I deeply respect your work in [specific area] and would love to learn from your expertise as I develop my career in [your focus area]," demonstrates sincerity and clarity.

- **Creating Learning Opportunities**

Learning opportunities are everywhere, but it takes a proactive mindset to capitalize on them. Here are some ways to integrate learning into your daily work routine:

1. On-the-job learning: Volunteer for challenging projects that stretch your skills. For instance, if you're a marketer, consider leading a campaign in an area you're less familiar with, such as analytics or social media strategy.

2. Upskilling programs: Enroll in online courses, webinars, or workshops tailored to your career aspirations.

These programs are often available through professional development platforms or industry-specific organizations.

3. Peer-to-peer learning: Collaborate with colleagues who have expertise in areas where you want to improve.

A graphic designer, for example, could learn basic coding from a web developer on the same team.

4. Feedback loops: Actively seek constructive feedback from your supervisors and peers.

For instance, after presenting a proposal, ask a trusted colleague for their honest opinion about what worked and what could improve.

- **Integrating Mentorship and Learning**

The most successful professionals seamlessly integrate mentorship with continuous learning.

For instance, if you've identified a gap in your skills during a mentorship session, take actionable steps to address it.

If your mentor suggests building your public speaking skills, enroll in a local workshop or join a speaking club.

Discuss your progress with your mentor during follow-ups to show commitment and seek additional guidance.

- **The Long-Term Impact**

Actively seeking mentorship and learning opportunities positions you as a high-potential individual within your organization.

It signals your willingness to grow and contribute to the team's success. Over time, these habits will build confidence, sharpen your skills, and create a network of allies who support your career trajectory.

STAYING RELEVANT IN A COMPETITIVE INDUSTRY

In an era of constant change and relentless competition, staying relevant at work isn't optional—it's essential.

Imagine being the go-to expert in your field, effortlessly navigating challenges, and consistently standing out from the crowd.

Whether you're just starting your career or looking to maintain your edge, this guide reveals practical, empowering habits that fuel workplace success.

From mastering adaptability to building a strong personal brand, these habits aren't just strategies—they're game-changers.

Learn how to embrace change, foster collaboration, and cultivate emotional intelligence to remain indispensable in your industry.

With relatable examples and actionable tips, you'll discover how to turn challenges into opportunities and setbacks into stepping stones.

Ready to secure your place at the forefront of your industry? Dive in and start building the future you deserve!

In today's ever-evolving work environment, staying relevant requires intentional habits that empower individuals to succeed.

The ability to adapt, learn, and lead within your industry determines your long-term viability.

Here's a look at some empowering habits for workplace success that ensure you remain indispensable in a competitive landscape.

1. Commit to Lifelong Learning

The most effective way to stay relevant is to continuously improve your skills and knowledge. Industries evolve, and so must you.

Enroll in professional courses, attend workshops, or read books and articles that expand your understanding of current trends.

For instance, if you're in the tech industry, keeping up with programming languages or emerging technologies like AI can set you apart.

- **Example:** A graphic designer who stays updated on the latest design software will outshine competitors using outdated tools.

Learning platforms like credible online academies and forums offer certifications that demonstrate your expertise.

2. Embrace Change and Adaptability

Change is constant, and those who resist it risk becoming obsolete. Being adaptable means anticipating change and preparing to pivot when necessary.

For example, during the rise of remote work, professionals who embraced virtual collaboration tools such as shared digital workspaces remained productive and relevant.

- Tip: Develop a mindset that views challenges as opportunities for growth. When your company introduces new policies or technologies, be among the first to master and champion them.

3. Build a Strong Personal Brand

In a competitive workplace, your reputation is your brand. Develop a professional identity that communicates reliability, expertise, and a willingness to go the extra mile.

A strong personal brand not only helps you stand out but also positions you as an authority in your field.

- **Example:** A sales representative who shares thought-provoking insights on industry trends via professional networking platforms establishes themselves as a thought leader.

This visibility can lead to career advancements or networking opportunities.

4. Cultivate Emotional Intelligence

Workplaces are not just about skills but also relationships. Emotional intelligence—understanding and managing your emotions and those of others—can make you an invaluable team member.

- **Tip:** Practice active listening, show empathy, and approach conflicts with a problem-solving mindset.

For instance, if a colleague struggles with deadlines, offering constructive feedback instead of criticism fosters collaboration and mutual respect.

5. Innovate and Take Initiative

Relevance often stems from innovation. Propose solutions to existing problems, streamline processes, or volunteer for projects outside your regular responsibilities.

Initiative shows that you're proactive, resourceful, and committed to organizational goals.

- **Example:** If you notice inefficiencies in your department's workflow, suggest using productivity-enhancing systems or methods. Being the person who identifies and resolves challenges boosts your value.

6. Network Strategically

Building a strong professional network keeps you informed about industry trends and opens doors to new opportunities.

Attend conferences, participate in online communities, and maintain relationships with mentors and colleagues.

- **Example:** A marketing professional who regularly connects with industry leaders at trade events might learn about upcoming shifts in consumer behavior before others, giving them a competitive edge.

7. Master Time Management

In a competitive industry, efficiency is non-negotiable. Organize your day to prioritize high-impact tasks while meeting deadlines. Use planners, productivity apps, or the classic to-do list to track progress.

- **Tip:** Avoid burnout by balancing work and personal life. Knowing when to take breaks can enhance focus and creativity, which are critical for staying ahead.

CHAPTER

11

THE ROLE OF SELF-CARE IN SUSTAINING SUCCESS

"Imagine this: You're a race car driver in the biggest competition of your life. Your car is a marvel of engineering—sleek, powerful, and built for speed.

But there's a catch: you never stop for fuel, ignore tire changes, and push the engine past its limits.

What happens? The car overheats, the tires blow, and you're left on the sidelines watching others zoom past you.

Now think of yourself as the driver and your body and mind as the car. Without self-care—your metaphorical pit stop—you risk burnout, fatigue, and a breakdown.

Success isn't about flooring the gas pedal at all times; it's about knowing when to pause, refuel, and recharge.

The most successful drivers (and professionals) make strategic pit stops to ensure they not only stay in the race but finish strong.

Ready to explore how self-care can be your ultimate performance strategy? Let's dive in!"

Self-care is not merely a trendy buzzword; it is a cornerstone for maintaining productivity, mental clarity, and overall well-being in the workplace.

Success is often associated with hard work, long hours, and relentless ambition, but these elements alone can lead to burnout if not balanced with intentional self-care practices.

Incorporating self-care into your routine is not a luxury—it's a necessity for sustaining long-term success.

- **Understanding Self-Care**

Self-care is the practice of deliberately taking time to care for your physical, mental, and emotional health.

It includes activities that rejuvenate you, relieve stress, and promote a healthy work-life balance.

Neglecting self-care in favor of work can create a vicious cycle of decreased productivity and increased stress.

- **Physical Self-Care: Energizing the Body**

Your physical health is the foundation of your ability to perform well in the workplace.

For instance, maintaining a regular exercise routine not only keeps you fit but also boosts energy levels and reduces stress.

A brisk 20-minute walk during lunch can clear your mind, leaving you refreshed for the afternoon.

Adequate sleep is another non-negotiable aspect of physical self-care.

Studies consistently show that lack of sleep impairs cognitive function, decision-making, and emotional regulation.

Successful individuals prioritize sleep as part of their routine, knowing that rest enhances focus and efficiency.

- **Mental Self-Care: Cultivating a Resilient Mind**

Mental self-care involves activities that help you stay focused, reduce stress, and foster creativity.

For example, mindfulness practices like meditation or deep-breathing exercises can help you manage workplace pressure.

Spending ten minutes in quiet reflection before tackling a challenging project can sharpen your focus and calm your mind.

Another aspect of mental self-care is setting boundaries. Saying "no" to additional responsibilities when your plate is full demonstrates an understanding of your limits and ensures the quality of your work remains high.

- **Emotional Self-Care: Building Inner Strength**

Emotional self-care is about nurturing your feelings and maintaining a positive mindset.

Taking breaks to connect with loved ones, expressing gratitude, or even indulging in a hobby can recharge your emotional batteries.

For instance, dedicating an hour on weekends to painting or gardening might seem unrelated to your professional goals, but it can restore your emotional balance, making you more effective at work.

Journaling is another practical tool for emotional self-care. Writing down your thoughts and reflections can help you process emotions, gain clarity, and develop self-awareness—key traits for navigating workplace challenges.

- **Self-Care as a Strategy for Success**

Consider the story of a high-achieving marketing professional who faced burnout after years of relentless work.

Recognizing the need for change, she began incorporating self-care practices such as morning yoga, unplugging from work emails after hours, and scheduling regular vacations.

Within months, her productivity improved, her creative problem-solving skills returned, and she found greater satisfaction in her career.

This example underscores a vital lesson: success is not about working harder, but about working smarter.

Self-care empowers you to sustain high performance by keeping you energized, focused, and emotionally balanced.

- **Practical Tips for Workplace Self-Care**

- **Plan Breaks:** Schedule short breaks throughout the day to stretch, hydrate, or simply step away from your desk.

- **Healthy Nutrition:** Keep nourishing snacks handy to maintain energy levels and focus.

- **Workspace Organization:** A tidy, well-organized workspace can reduce stress and enhance efficiency.

- **Time Management:** Use tools like digital planners to prioritize tasks and avoid last-minute scrambles.

- **Celebrate Small Wins:** Acknowledge your achievements, no matter how small, to keep motivation high.

- **The Bigger Picture**

Ultimately, self-care is about honoring your personal needs so that you can perform at your best.

THE IMPACT OF PHYSICAL HEALTH ON PERFORMANCE

Your body is the engine of your ambition—fuel it with health, and you'll power through challenges with focus, energy, and resilience.

Neglect it, and even the brightest dreams will dim under the weight of fatigue and stress.

Physical health plays a pivotal role in shaping workplace performance. A healthy body fuels a productive mind, allowing individuals to tackle tasks with energy and focus.

Neglecting physical well-being, on the other hand, often leads to reduced efficiency, fatigue, and an increased likelihood of errors.

In the context of empowering habits for workplace success, maintaining physical health should be a non-negotiable priority.

- **Enhanced Energy and Stamina**

When employees prioritize their physical health, they are better equipped to handle demanding workdays.

Regular exercise, balanced nutrition, and adequate sleep serve as the foundation for sustained energy levels.

For instance, incorporating a 30-minute walk or light exercise routine into the day can enhance blood flow, which boosts energy and cognitive function.

A well-nourished body is less prone to mid-day energy crashes, enabling individuals to remain productive throughout the day.

- **Improved Mental Clarity and Focus**

Physical health directly influences mental performance. Regular physical activity has been shown to reduce stress hormones like cortisol and increase endorphins, leading to improved mood and sharper focus.

A well-balanced diet rich in essential nutrients, such as omega-3 fatty acids and antioxidants, supports brain health and enhances cognitive function.

Employees who invest in their physical well-being often find themselves better equipped to manage complex tasks, make informed decisions, and think creatively.

- **Reduced Absenteeism**

Employees in good physical health are less likely to fall ill and miss work. Preventive care, such as maintaining an active lifestyle and managing weight, can reduce the risk of chronic conditions like diabetes, hypertension, and heart disease.

This not only benefits the individual but also the organization, as lower absenteeism rates translate into increased consistency and team collaboration.

- **Increased Resilience and Stress Management**

A healthy body is better prepared to handle stress. Regular physical activity helps regulate stress responses, making it easier to navigate high-pressure situations at work.

Deep breathing exercises, yoga, or even a short walk during breaks can be transformative in managing stress levels.

Employees who integrate such habits into their routine demonstrate greater resilience and adaptability, traits essential for thriving in dynamic workplaces.

- **Practical Steps to Prioritize Physical Health in the Workplace**

1. Incorporate Movement: Encourage short movement breaks during the workday, whether through stretching, walking, or light exercise.

2. Promote Healthy Eating: Replace processed snacks with options like fruits, nuts, or whole grains to boost energy levels naturally.

3. Emphasize Rest: Advocate for proper sleep hygiene and discourage overworking to prevent burnout.

4. Support Wellness Programs: Offer or participate in workplace wellness initiatives to foster a culture of health.

SUPPORTING MENTAL WELLNESS

Success in the workplace isn't just about the tasks you complete but the mindset you cultivate.

When you prioritize mental wellness, you unlock the resilience to face challenges, the clarity to make better decisions, and the emotional strength to build meaningful connections.

A thriving mind isn't just a tool for productivity—it's the foundation of a fulfilling and impactful career.

Mental wellness is a cornerstone of achieving long-term success in the workplace.

A healthy mind promotes productivity, creativity, and resilience, enabling individuals to navigate challenges with clarity and confidence.

Integrating habits that support mental well-being into daily routines can profoundly impact workplace performance and overall satisfaction.

1. Prioritize Emotional Intelligence
Understanding and managing your emotions while empathizing with others is essential in the workplace.

Emotional intelligence (EQ) fosters effective communication, reduces conflicts, and strengthens team dynamics. Develop this skill by:

- ❖ Practicing mindfulness to recognize your emotional triggers.

- ❖ Actively listening to colleagues without judgment.

- ❖ Offering constructive feedback with empathy.

2. Set Boundaries for a Healthy Work-Life Balance

Balancing professional responsibilities with personal time is critical for mental wellness.

Constantly being "on" can lead to burnout, reduced efficiency, and emotional fatigue. To create a healthier balance:

- ❖ Establish clear work hours and stick to them.

- ❖ Take short, restorative breaks throughout the day.

- ❖ Communicate your boundaries clearly to colleagues and supervisors.

3. Incorporate Regular Movement

Physical activity has a direct impact on mental health by reducing stress, boosting mood, and increasing energy levels. You don't need a gym membership or elaborate equipment to stay active:

- ❖ Take a 10-minute walk during lunch breaks.

- ❖ Stretch or practice simple yoga poses at your desk.

- ❖ Use stairs instead of elevators whenever possible.

4. Foster Supportive Workplace Relationships

Positive connections with colleagues can create a more inclusive, collaborative, and mentally uplifting environment. Build these connections by:

- ❖ Participating in team-building activities.

- ❖ Showing appreciation for coworkers' contributions.

- ❖ Offering help or mentorship to those who need it.

5. Cultivate a Growth Mindset

A growth mindset encourages individuals to view challenges as opportunities for learning rather than obstacles.

This approach can reduce anxiety and promote resilience in the face of workplace pressures. Develop this mindset by:

- ❖ Celebrating small successes as stepping stones to larger goals.

- ❖ Seeking feedback and using it constructively.

- ❖ Viewing mistakes as valuable learning experiences.

6. Leverage Stress Management Techniques

Workplace stress is inevitable, but managing it effectively can safeguard mental wellness. Techniques to handle stress include:

- ❖ Practicing deep breathing or meditation for relaxation.

- ❖ Breaking down tasks into smaller, manageable steps.

- ❖ Using visualization techniques to create a sense of calm.

7. Focus on Nutrition and Hydration

The foods you consume directly affect your mood, energy levels, and cognitive function. Prioritize mental wellness by:

- ❖ Eating nutrient-rich foods, such as whole grains, lean proteins, and vegetables.

- Drinking water consistently to stay hydrated.

- Avoiding excessive caffeine and processed snacks.

8. Practice Gratitude

Gratitude can shift your mindset, improve relationships, and reduce workplace tension. Incorporate gratitude into your day by:

- Reflecting on three positive events from your workday.

- Writing thank-you notes to coworkers.

- Celebrating achievements, big or small.

9. Normalize Conversations About Mental Health

Creating an environment where discussing mental health is not stigmatized encourages individuals to seek help when needed. Contribute to this cultural shift by:

- ❖ Sharing resources for counseling or support services.

- ❖ Encouraging open dialogue about mental health in team meetings.

- ❖ Leading by example by acknowledging your own mental wellness practices.

BALANCING WORK AND PERSONAL GROWTH

True success is not measured by the hours you dedicate to work but by the balance you create between advancing your career and nurturing your soul.

When you align your ambitions with personal growth, you don't just achieve—you thrive.

Achieving a balance between work responsibilities and personal growth is one of the most vital aspects of professional and personal success.

This equilibrium fosters not only a fulfilling career but also personal development that enhances overall well-being.

Below are actionable strategies to help balance these two essential areas.

1. Prioritize Time Management

One of the primary challenges in balancing work and personal growth is effectively managing time.

Establishing a clear schedule that delineates work tasks and personal development activities ensures neither aspect is neglected.

For instance, you might dedicate mornings to creative endeavors like journaling or skill-building before starting your workday.

Similarly, setting aside specific hours for work-related tasks eliminates the temptation to let work encroach on personal time.

Instance:

A marketing professional, Sarah, struggled to find time for her passion for painting.

By reserving Saturday mornings exclusively for her art, she not only improved her painting skills but also returned to work on Mondays feeling refreshed and inspired.

2. Set Clear Boundaries

In today's interconnected world, the lines between work and personal life often blur, especially when working remotely.

Setting clear boundaries, such as avoiding work emails after a designated hour or turning off notifications during personal growth activities, ensures that your attention is fully present in each sphere.

Instance:

John, a software engineer, made it a habit to put his phone on "Do Not Disturb" mode during his evening yoga sessions.

This boundary not only improved his physical health but also helped him mentally recharge for demanding projects at work.

3. Develop Growth-Oriented Goals

Personal growth flourishes when it is tied to clear, actionable goals. These could include learning a new skill, engaging in hobbies, or pursuing further education.

Aligning these goals with your professional aspirations creates a synergy between work and personal growth.

For instance, improving public speaking through community events can also benefit workplace presentations.

Instance:

Emma, an HR manager, joined a local book club to improve her critical thinking and interpersonal skills.

Over time, this contributed to her ability to mediate complex workplace issues, benefiting both her career and personal growth.

4. Leverage Micro-Habits

Building micro-habits—small, incremental changes—can lead to significant long-term personal and professional development.

For example, reading ten pages of a professional book each night, practicing mindfulness for five minutes, or dedicating ten minutes daily to a new language can have transformative effects without overwhelming your schedule.

Instance:

Daniel, an entry-level accountant, began dedicating just five minutes daily to learning coding basics.

Within six months, this micro-habit opened opportunities for him to transition into a hybrid role that combined accounting and automation.

5. Incorporate Wellness Practices

Personal growth often stems from mental and physical well-being. Incorporating wellness practices such as regular exercise, proper nutrition, and mindfulness can significantly enhance both work productivity and personal satisfaction.

Instance:

Leila, a teacher, found herself overwhelmed with grading and lesson planning.

By committing to a 20-minute daily meditation routine, she improved her focus and reduced burnout, allowing her to be more effective in her role and personal life.

6. Seek Supportive Environments

Both work and personal growth thrive in supportive environments. Seek out workplaces that encourage professional development, foster work-life balance, and offer mentorship opportunities.

Similarly, surround yourself with friends and family who support your growth journey.

Instance:

Adam, a graphic designer, joined a company that offered monthly creative workshops.

These sessions allowed him to explore new design trends while also networking with like-minded individuals, enriching both his career and personal life.

7. Reflect and Reassess

Finally, regular self-reflection ensures that you stay on track with your goals. Reassess your priorities and adjust your routines to align with your evolving aspirations.

Instance:

Maya, a project manager, revisits her goals every quarter. This habit has allowed her to adapt her personal growth strategies to her changing career demands, ensuring continuous improvement.

Balancing work and personal growth is not a one-size-fits-all approach. By implementing these strategies and tailoring them to your unique circumstances, you can create a harmonious balance that fuels both professional success and personal fulfillment.

Remember, empowering habits are the foundation of sustainable workplace success.

CHAPTER

12

BUILDING HABITS THAT LAST

The concept of habits has shaped human achievement for centuries. Ancient Greek philosophers said that excellence was not a single act but a habit cultivated through repeated action.

Fast forward to modern times, many leaders attribute their success to the consistency of small daily actions.

For instance, a celebrated American polymath, renowned for his diverse achievements, practiced a rigorous routine to master virtues such as discipline and focus.

This legacy of habit formation underscores the importance of habits in achieving sustained workplace success.

In the workplace, habits are the invisible architecture of our daily productivity.

From how we approach our tasks to how we interact with colleagues, our habits either propel us toward our goals or hold us back.

Understanding the power of habits and building those that align with professional goals is essential for empowerment and growth.

To build habits that last, especially for workplace success, it's important to focus on small, meaningful actions and maintain consistency.

Sustainable habits are not born overnight; they are nurtured over time with intention and perseverance.

1. Start Small and Specific

Instead of overhauling your entire routine, begin with one specific habit that directly impacts your work.

For example, if you struggle with time management, start by dedicating the first 10 minutes of your day to planning your tasks.

This small action builds a foundation for better time management without feeling overwhelming.

2. Create Triggers for Consistency

Triggers act as cues that remind you to perform a habit. For instance, pairing a habit with an existing routine can reinforce it.

If you want to improve communication with your team, make it a habit to send a brief update email right after your morning coffee.

Associating the habit with an established routine makes it easier to remember and execute.

3. Measure Progress and Reward Success

Tracking progress helps reinforce positive habits. For example, keep a simple checklist or journal to note each time you complete your new habit.

Pair this with small, meaningful rewards. If you successfully complete your habit for a week, treat yourself to something you enjoy.

This combination of progress tracking and rewards strengthens the habit loop.

4. Focus on Identity, Not Just Actions

Sustainable habits come from aligning them with your professional identity.

Instead of saying, "I want to be more organized," reframe it as, "I am a person who values organization."

This subtle shift focuses on who you are becoming rather than just what you're doing.

5. Adapt to Challenges

Workplace environments are dynamic, and challenges are inevitable. When setbacks occur, avoid perfectionism.

If you miss a habit one day, recommit to it the next. Building resilience in the face of inconsistency ensures that your habits withstand obstacles.

- **Practical Examples of Workplace Habits**

- Time Management: Schedule a daily 15-minute review of your tasks. This habit keeps priorities clear and prevents procrastination.

- Professional Development: Dedicate 30 minutes twice a week to learning a new skill related to your field.

This small habit compounds over time, making you more competent and competitive.

- Networking: Make it a habit to reach out to one colleague or industry peer every week. Over time, this practice builds a strong professional network.

- Health and Wellness: Stand up and stretch for 5 minutes every hour. This simple habit boosts productivity and prevents burnout.

- **Empowering Yourself Through Habits**

Building habits that last is not just about individual actions; it's about creating a framework for consistent growth.

As you develop empowering habits for workplace success, remember the words of a prominent historian, summarizing an ancient

Greek philosopher: "We are what we repeatedly do. Excellence, then, is not an act but a habit."

Start small, stay consistent, and watch as your habits transform not only your workplace performance but also your professional identity.

STRATEGIES FOR MAINTAINING POSITIVE CHANGES

you're at the helm of a ship sailing toward an island of success. The waters are calm, the breeze is just right, and the compass—your goals—is guiding you steadily.

Suddenly, storm clouds appear on the horizon, the waves get choppy, and you lose sight of the island.

Do you give up and let the sea carry you wherever it wants? Or do you adjust your sails, double-check your compass, and navigate with even greater determination?

This is the essence of maintaining positive habits in the workplace. Like navigating a ship, sustaining your empowering habits requires clear direction, a supportive crew, and tools to weather inevitable storms.

Whether it's using habit-stacking to reinforce your routine, celebrating small victories like finding calmer waters, or re-charting your course when obstacles arise, these strategies ensure you keep moving forward.

Imagine the rewards of staying on course—reaching that island of success with a treasure chest of confidence, productivity, and career growth.

The journey may have its challenges, but with the right mindset and tools, your ship is unstoppable.

Ready to take the wheel? Dive in to discover how to keep your habits thriving and your career soaring!

Adopting empowering habits for workplace success is an excellent start, but sustaining these positive changes requires intentional strategies.

Here are key methods to ensure long-term success in maintaining these habits, complete with practical examples.

1. Set Clear Goals and Measure Progress
Establish specific, measurable objectives for the habits you want to sustain.

Break these goals into manageable milestones and track your progress regularly.

Instance: If you aim to improve time management, set a goal to reduce wasted time during meetings by 30% over the next month.

Use tools like checklists or simple spreadsheets to measure how effectively meetings stay on track.

2. Create an Accountability System

Accountability is crucial in forming long-lasting habits. Share your goals with a colleague, mentor, or even a group of coworkers who can help keep you on track.

Instance: If you're working on improving workplace communication, ask a trusted colleague to give you feedback after team discussions or presentations.

3. Leverage Habit Stacking

Habit stacking involves attaching a new habit to an already established one. This approach makes integrating new habits into your routine more seamless.

Instance: If you're cultivating the habit of daily learning, you can combine it with your lunch break.

Commit to reading a professional article or watching an industry-related video as you eat.

4. Reward Yourself for Progress

Positive reinforcement strengthens the likelihood of maintaining new behaviors. Celebrate small wins and acknowledge progress to stay motivated.

Instance: If you consistently meet deadlines for a month, treat yourself to something enjoyable, like a book, a special dinner, or an extra hour of relaxation on the weekend.

5. Anticipate and Manage Obstacles

Identify potential challenges that could disrupt your progress and have a plan to address them. Prepare alternative actions to stay on track during difficult periods.

Instance: If you struggle to maintain focus during high-pressure weeks, use productivity techniques like setting shorter, focused work sessions or delegating less critical tasks to team members.

6. Cultivate a Growth Mindset

A growth mindset helps you see setbacks as opportunities for learning rather than failures.

This perspective is essential for maintaining positive changes over time.

Instance: If you miss a weekly goal, analyze the reasons behind it and adjust your approach for the next week instead of giving up entirely.

7. Build a Supportive Environment

Your surroundings influence your habits. Design a work environment that encourages positive behavior and minimizes distractions.

Instance: If you're working on staying organized, declutter your workspace and keep only essential tools or files within easy reach. This makes sticking to organizational habits easier.

8. Regularly Reassess and Adapt

Periodic reassessment ensures that your habits align with your evolving goals and workplace demands. Be willing to adapt as circumstances change.

Instance: If a habit like prioritizing tasks no longer fits your expanded responsibilities, refine it by using a system like task categorization to address high-priority and low-priority items differently.

9. Stay Inspired and Educated

Constant learning keeps you motivated and helps reinforce positive changes. Attend workshops, read books, or join professional communities to stay inspired.

Instance: If you're focused on improving leadership skills, participate in webinars or join a management forum to learn from peers and experts.

10. Practice Self-Care and Resilience

A healthy body and mind are critical for sustaining workplace habits. Incorporate activities like regular exercise, mindfulness, and sufficient sleep to maintain your energy and focus.

Instance: Schedule 15 minutes daily for meditation or deep breathing exercises to manage stress and improve clarity during busy workdays.

Maintaining positive changes in the workplace requires commitment, flexibility, and a proactive approach.

OVERCOMING CHALLENGES IN HABIT FORMATION

What separates high achievers from the rest in the workplace? It's not just talent or opportunity—it's the habits they cultivate every single day.

But let's be honest: forming new habits is easier said than done. If you've ever tried to make a positive change and felt stuck, distracted, or unmotivated, you're not alone.

In *Overcoming Challenges in Habit Formation*, we explore practical solutions to the most common obstacles that prevent you from building habits that fuel success.

From battling procrastination to overcoming workplace distractions, this guide is packed with actionable strategies you can start using immediately.

Imagine starting your day with a clear focus, tackling your most important tasks without hesitation, and creating routines that make you stand out in your field.

Whether you're looking to enhance productivity, improve communication, or maintain consistency despite setbacks, this piece has you covered.

Dive in and discover how small, intentional changes can transform your workday—and your career. Let this be your roadmap to building empowering habits that truly stick.

Forming empowering habits is a cornerstone for workplace success, yet the journey is often riddled with challenges.

Understanding these challenges and learning how to overcome them can make all the difference in cultivating habits that propel your professional growth.

1. Understanding Resistance to Change

One of the primary challenges in habit formation is resistance to change. Our brains are wired to favor the familiar, making it difficult to adopt new behaviors.

For example, if you're trying to establish a habit of starting your workday with focused planning, the pull to dive directly into emails can derail you.

Solution:

Start small. Begin with a two-minute habit of jotting down your top priorities before tackling your inbox. This minimal effort reduces resistance and helps your brain adapt gradually.

2. The Trap of Instant Gratification

Workplace habits often require delaying gratification, a significant hurdle.

For instance, the habit of maintaining detailed project notes may feel tedious, especially when there's no immediate reward.

However, neglecting this habit can lead to confusion and missed deadlines later.

Solution:

Tie the habit to a short-term reward. After completing your project notes, treat yourself to a five-minute break or a cup of coffee. Associating a small reward with the task can motivate you to stick with it.

3. Overcoming Procrastination

Procrastination is another barrier to habit formation. It often stems from the fear of failure or the overwhelming nature of starting a new habit.

For instance, developing the habit of proactive communication might be daunting if you're unsure how to approach difficult conversations with colleagues.

Solution:
Break the habit into smaller steps. Instead of focusing on mastering proactive communication overnight, commit to sending one well-thought-out email or scheduling one check-in meeting per week. Gradually increase your efforts as your confidence grows.

4. Dealing with Setbacks
Setbacks are inevitable when forming habits. Missing a day or two of a new practice, such as

a morning routine to prepare for meetings, can feel like failure and lead to giving up entirely.

Solution:

Adopt a growth mindset. Remind yourself that progress, not perfection, is the goal.

Acknowledge the setback, analyze its cause, and resume your habit the next day. Consistency over time matters more than daily perfection.

5. Navigating Workplace Distractions

Workplaces are often bustling environments with constant distractions, making it challenging to stick to habits.

For instance, building a habit of deep work might be interrupted by frequent meetings or unplanned requests.

Solution:

Create boundaries. Allocate specific blocks of time for focused tasks and communicate your availability to your team.

Use tools like calendar blocks or "do not disturb" settings to safeguard these periods.

6. Staying Motivated During Plateaus

Once the novelty of a habit fades, motivation can wane. This often happens after initial progress when the habit starts to feel monotonous.

For example, if you're cultivating the habit of continuous learning by dedicating time to read industry updates, it may become less exciting over time.

Solution:

Reframe the habit as an investment. Remind yourself of the long-term benefits, such as increased expertise or career advancement.

Additionally, switch up your routine by exploring new sources of information, like podcasts or webinars, to keep things fresh.

7. Balancing Competing Priorities
Workplace demands can often clash with personal goals, making it difficult to maintain habits.

For instance, balancing the habit of taking a midday walk to recharge with a packed meeting schedule can feel impossible.

Solution:
Integrate habits into existing routines. Instead of a midday walk, try walking during a phone call or using stairs instead of elevators.

Embedding habits into your day minimizes additional time commitments.

Overcoming challenges in habit formation is a skill that requires patience, strategy, and persistence.

CELEBRATING WINS TO STAY MOTIVATED

How can celebrating small wins at work transform your motivation and boost long-term success?

Celebrating small wins creates a ripple effect of positivity in the workplace. It reinforces good habits, strengthens team morale, and sustains motivation for long-term goals.

Whether it's acknowledging personal progress, publicly recognizing a colleague's contribution, or organizing a group celebration, these moments of recognition remind you and your team of the value in every step forward.

By making celebration a habit, you cultivate a culture of success and ensure that progress remains a powerful motivator on your journey to excellence.

Success in the workplace is not just about hitting targets or achieving goals; it's about recognizing and celebrating progress along the way.

Celebrating wins, whether big or small, is a powerful habit that boosts morale, reinforces positive behavior, and keeps motivation levels high.

By acknowledging achievements, we create a sense of accomplishment that drives future efforts. Here's how to integrate this empowering habit into your professional life effectively.

- **Why Celebrating Wins Matters**

1. Reinforces Positive Behavior
Acknowledging success, no matter how minor, reinforces the behaviors and habits that led to the achievement.

For example, if a team successfully completes a challenging project ahead of schedule, celebrating the milestone highlights the collaboration and dedication that made it possible. This encouragement fosters a culture of excellence and repeated success.

2. Boosts Team Morale
In fast-paced work environments, it's easy to focus solely on the next task without pausing to appreciate what has been accomplished.

Recognizing wins—like landing a new client or resolving a critical issue—brings a sense of fulfillment, reminding everyone of the value they contribute to the organization. High morale leads to higher productivity and a more cohesive team.

3. Sustains Long-Term Motivation

Big goals often require sustained effort over extended periods. Celebrating small wins along the way helps maintain momentum.

For instance, if you're working on a year-long sales target, celebrating quarterly progress ensures you and your team stay motivated to push forward.

- **How to Celebrate Wins Effectively**

1. Personal Acknowledgment

Celebrate your own wins by taking a moment to reflect on what went well.

Write down your achievements in a journal or share them with a colleague or mentor.

For example, if you presented a successful proposal that secured funding, treat yourself to a meaningful reward like a nice meal or a day off to recharge.

2. Public Recognition

In team settings, public recognition works wonders. A simple mention during a meeting, a congratulatory email, or even a physical note of appreciation can make people feel valued.

For instance, a team leader might highlight an employee's innovative solution to a problem during a department-wide meeting.

3. Celebrate as a Group

For team achievements, organize a group celebration. This could be as simple as a shared lunch or as elaborate as an off-site event, depending on the scale of the success.

For example, if the marketing team achieves a record-breaking campaign performance, a celebratory team outing can build camaraderie and strengthen bonds.

4. Visual Reminders of Success

Consider creating a success board in the office or a virtual equivalent for remote teams.

Document achievements like reaching milestones, surpassing targets, or completing significant projects.

Seeing these accomplishments displayed serves as a constant reminder of progress and inspires further success.

- **Instances of Celebrating Wins**

❖ **- Small Wins:**
Imagine you've been struggling to adopt a new productivity tool. After weeks of learning and experimenting, you finally master it and see improvements in your workflow.

Celebrate by acknowledging your growth and sharing your experience with peers who might benefit from it.

❖ **- Team Milestones:**
When a department transitions to a new operational system with minimal disruption, it's a moment worth celebrating.

A short coffee break where team members share their experiences and challenges can be both rewarding and insightful.

❖ **- Personal Goals:**

After working tirelessly to improve your public speaking skills, you deliver a flawless presentation at a major conference.

Reflect on how far you've come and reward yourself with something you enjoy, like attending a concert or purchasing that book you've been eyeing.

- **Building a Culture of Celebration**

To make celebrating a consistent habit, integrate it into your workplace culture.

Encourage leaders to model the behavior by regularly recognizing efforts.

Create systems for peer-to-peer recognition, where colleagues can acknowledge each other's contributions.

For example, a weekly "shout-out" session during meetings can highlight individual and team achievements.

Incorporating celebrations into your workflow doesn't require significant resources—it only requires intentionality.

By celebrating wins regularly, you'll not only stay motivated but also inspire those around you to strive for success.

This simple but powerful habit ensures that progress, not just perfection, remains at the forefront of your journey to workplace success.

CONCLUSION

Your Path to Workplace Success

Imagine waking up each day with a clear purpose, knowing you have the tools to conquer challenges and seize opportunities.

What if your workplace wasn't just a place to clock in but a stage for your growth, creativity, and success? This isn't just a dream—it's a reality within your reach.

In *Empowering Habits for Workplace Success,* you'll uncover the practical strategies that transform ambition into achievement.

These habits are more than ideas; they're actionable steps that have the power to reshape your professional journey.

From building strong connections to mastering resilience, this book equips you to thrive in any environment.

Ready to take control of your future? The path to workplace success is in your hands.

Start now, and make every day a step closer to the career and life you've always envisioned. Turn the page, and take the leap—you're worth it.

As we wrap up this exploration of *Empowering Habits for Workplace Success,* you now hold the tools to transform your professional life.

The habits we've discussed aren't just theoretical concepts—they are proven strategies to elevate your career, enhance your relationships, and boost your productivity in meaningful ways.

By cultivating consistency, communication, and creativity, you empower yourself to thrive in any environment.

When you prioritize personal growth, embrace accountability, and foster adaptability, you lay the groundwork for a career filled with purpose and accomplishment.

Remember, true success isn't a destination—it's a journey of continual improvement, driven by the habits you choose to adopt today.

Take ownership of your potential and lead with confidence, focus, and integrity. The path to workplace success begins with intentional action and a commitment to excellence.

You have the power to shape your future—so take the first step, and let these empowering habits guide you to a thriving and fulfilling professional life. The best is yet to come.

THE POWER OF CONSISTENCY AND COMMITMENT

Success in the workplace is not built on fleeting moments of brilliance but on the quiet, steadfast rhythm of consistent effort and unwavering commitment.

It is the daily choice to show up, do the work, and stay the course that true excellence takes root, transforming ordinary habits into extraordinary achievements.

The power of consistency and commitment plays a transformative role in cultivating habits that lead to workplace success.

At its core, consistency is about showing up every day with purpose, regardless of obstacles. It's the quiet force that builds trust, reinforces dependability, and creates a foundation for long-term achievement.

In a professional environment, where reliability is often as valuable as talent, the consistent delivery of quality work strengthens relationships and opens doors to new opportunities.

Commitment, on the other hand, is the fuel that sustains consistency. It embodies the deep-rooted determination to follow through, even when the path becomes challenging.

In the workplace, commitment translates into perseverance during tight deadlines, the willingness to embrace feedback for growth, and a proactive attitude toward personal and team objectives.

A committed professional doesn't merely complete tasks but approaches them with an intrinsic drive to excel and contribute meaningfully.

When consistency and commitment are combined, they foster a sense of accountability that sets a person apart.

Colleagues and supervisors recognize the dependable rhythm of your efforts, which instills confidence in your capabilities.

This duo also reinforces the power of habit, where small, intentional actions performed daily can lead to extraordinary outcomes.

Whether it's consistently arriving prepared for meetings, dedicating focused time to skill development, or staying aligned with company values, these habits shape a career narrative that speaks volumes about professionalism and reliability.

Beyond individual impact, consistency and commitment influence workplace culture. They inspire others to adopt similar habits, creating an environment where collaboration thrives, and goals are achieved collectively.

A team built on shared commitment operates with greater cohesion and purpose, as each member's reliability strengthens the group's collective output.

In the journey toward workplace success, the mastery of empowering habits lies not in sporadic bursts of effort but in the steady, unwavering application of energy and focus.

Consistency and commitment are not mere traits but intentional choices that shape the trajectory of a career.

By embracing these principles, professionals position themselves as resilient and indispensable contributors to their organizations.

EMBRACING THE JOURNEY OF GROWTH

Success in the workplace isn't about reaching a final destination; it's about mastering the art of growth—where adaptability fuels resilience, communication builds bridges, and every challenge becomes a stepping stone toward a stronger, more empowered version of yourself.

The workplace is not just a space for fulfilling professional responsibilities; it's a dynamic environment where individuals can embrace personal and professional growth.

Success in this realm is shaped by habits that empower employees to thrive in ever-changing landscapes.

Building these habits requires intentionality, consistency, and a commitment to self-improvement.

At the heart of workplace success is the ability to foster meaningful communication.

This isn't just about speaking or writing effectively; it's about truly listening, understanding diverse perspectives, and tailoring your approach to connect with colleagues and clients.

Effective communication builds trust and strengthens collaboration, paving the way for shared achievements.

Another cornerstone is adaptability. The modern workplace evolves rapidly, and those who can adjust their strategies and mindset are better positioned to succeed.

Being open to feedback, learning from setbacks, and embracing new challenges ensures that growth becomes a continuous journey rather than a destination.

Time management is equally vital. Prioritizing tasks, setting realistic goals, and maintaining focus amid distractions can transform overwhelming workloads into manageable accomplishments.

Developing a proactive mindset, where tasks are tackled with clarity and purpose, creates a sense of control and achievement.

Equally important is cultivating a growth mindset. Viewing challenges as opportunities to learn rather than obstacles to fear encourages resilience.

This perspective shifts the focus from avoiding failure to gaining insights from experiences, allowing for steady personal and professional improvement.

Finally, workplace success is deeply rooted in interpersonal relationships. Building genuine connections with colleagues fosters a supportive environment where collaboration flourishes.

Mutual respect, empathy, and shared goals create a sense of community that amplifies individual contributions.

Embracing these empowering habits is not an overnight transformation but a commitment to the journey of growth.

By integrating them into daily routines and maintaining a focus on self-development, workplace success becomes a natural extension of personal evolution.

ACKNOWLEDGMENTS

This book is the culmination of countless moments of support, inspiration, and guidance from many incredible individuals.

I am deeply grateful to those who have stood by me, shared their insights, and encouraged this journey to fruition.

To my family, thank you for your unwavering belief in my ability to bring this vision to life. Your love, patience, and understanding were the cornerstone of my resilience during long hours of writing and research.

To my close friends, your uplifting words and constant cheerleading helped me push forward when the road seemed tough.

I extend my heartfelt gratitude to my professional mentors and colleagues, whose wisdom and shared experiences enriched the content of this book.

Your real-world advice and examples illuminate the principles of success that so many readers will find valuable.

To my editor, your sharp eye and constructive feedback transformed ideas into a cohesive and impactful message.

Thank you for your dedication and for helping me craft a book that resonates with readers.

A special thanks goes to the many workplace professionals, leaders, and innovators who inspired sections of this book through their stories of success, challenges, and resilience.

Your experiences serve as powerful testaments to the habits that drive achievement.

Finally, to you, the reader—thank you for choosing to embark on this journey of growth and empowerment.

This book is for you, and I hope it serves as a valuable resource on your path to professional success.

Your willingness to embrace change, develop impactful habits, and strive for excellence is the true heartbeat of this work.

With gratitude,
[SCOTT E SALSBURY]

ABOUT THE AUTHOR

Scott E. Salsbury is a prominent author and esteemed leadership authority, committed to fostering personal and organizational growth.

With a Doctorate in Psychology, Scott combines his deep understanding of human behavior with practical insights to craft transformative strategies in leadership, self-help, business, and finance.

Scott has collaborated with numerous global organizations, providing customized training solutions for leadership enhancement and individual development.

His groundbreaking methodology has inspired numerous leaders and cultivated a culture of trust and collaboration.

With captivating narratives and applicable frameworks, Scott's books equip readers with essential skills for success in today's complex business environment.

He advocates that genuine leadership stems from authenticity and the capacity to motivate others, rendering his work both accessible and influential.

As a renowned thought leader, Scott dedicates himself to disseminating expertise through speaking, workshops, and coaching, cultivating a legacy of inspired leaders equipped for future challenges.

BOOKS OF THE AUTHOR

1. Path to purposeful leadership
2. Leading with trust and teamwork
3. Succeeding in hard times
4. Succeeding with goal challenges
5. Transforming self criticism into self compassion
6. Mindful living essential
7. The essential guide to power and influence
8. The skills that shape success
9. The path to influence and persuasion
10. Insight into the power of behavior
11. Success Habits For Aspiring Leaders
12. Skills for motivating teams effectively
13. Effective mindset change for leaders

www.ingramcontent.com/pod-product-compliance
Lightning Source LLC
Chambersburg PA
CBHW052138220526
45471CB00004B/1424